Dealing
With the
DAD
of
Your Past

Dealing
With the
DAD
of
Your Past

MAUREEN RANK

BETHANY HOUSE PUBLISHERS
MINNEAPOLIS, MINNESOTA 55438

Verses marked TLB are taken from *The Living Bible*, © 1971 by Tyndale House Publishers, Wheaton, Ill. Used by permission.

Verses marked NIV are from the Holy Bible, New International Version. Copyright © 1973, 1978, International Bible Society. Used by permission of Zondervan Bible Publishers.

Verses marked AMP are from the Amplified Bible. Old Testament copyright © 1965, 1987 by the Zondervan Corporation. The Amplified New Testament copyright © 1958, 1987 by the Lockman Foundation. Used by permission.

Published by Bethany House Publishers
A Ministry of Bethany Fellowship, Inc.
6820 Auto Club Road, Minneapolis, Minnesota 55438

Printed in the United States of America

Library of Congress Cataloging-in-Publication Data

Rank, Maureen.
    Dealing with the dad of your past / Maureen Rank.
       p. cm.
    Includes bibliographical references.

    1. Christian women—Religious life. 2. Women—Psychology.
3. Fathers and daughters. 4. Fatherhood (Christian theology)
5. God—Fatherhood. I. Title.
BV4527.R35   1990
248.8'43—dc20   90–40891
ISBN 0–87123–622–2   CIP

In honor of my parents,
Maurice and Ada Johnston,
who taught me to take chances.

MAUREEN RANK is a graduate of Iowa State University and spent six years on the Navigators' staff ministering to college students. She is author of seven books, including *God Can Make It Happen* and *Free to Grieve*. She and her husband live in Knoxville, Iowa, and have two children.

Contents

Introduction

You may be a part of what sociologists are calling "The Fatherless Generation." They've observed that in the years after World War II, the American father has become a vanishing species.

As divorce rates have spiraled, so have the number of children growing up in homes without a dad present. Currently, almost one-fourth of American children under age 18—some 10,000,000 kids—are growing up in fatherless families.

There is another kind of father-absence that doesn't show up in statistics like these, but the psychological effects of it can be almost as damaging as Dad's actual physical exit from the home, which began in the United States in massive proportions after World War II. With the incredible prosperity that swept America in the 1950s, Dad left for the office, bent on bringing home a sizable hunk of the American Dream. He worked twelve-hour days. He took to the road. He came home with a bulging briefcase, drained emotionally. Dad was still physically present, but emotionally absent, lost to a world of work that claimed all his time and energy. A significant portion of the children living in homes the demographic experts would describe as father-present actually experienced little or no fathers. We are still reeling from the effects of this present/ absence.

All right. So this generation has been blighted by fatherlessness. And doesn't the saying go, "Like mother, like daughter"?

But this book is written for women.

Perhaps you're thinking, "Wasn't it my mother whose impact mattered most in my development? As long as she was there, does it matter so much who my father was to me?"

Though you'd hardly know it from the direction most psychological research has taken in the last few decades, it does matter. Pokings into parent-child relationships have in many cases lumped both Mom and Dad together in a generic "parents" category, under several false assumptions: either that both of them behaved similarly toward their child, or that their impacts on the child's development were pretty much interchangeable. If only one parent was studied, it was nearly always the mother. And if Dad got his moment in the spotlight, his influence was most often evaluated as it affected his son, not his daughter. So any thought at all given to the influence of a dad on his daughter's development emerges as a relatively recent phenomenon.

But those who are studying the father-daughter relationship are coming out with some stunning conclusions. If what they are saying is true, a dad has a profound and lasting impact on his daughter's life.

We're slowly being nudged into a retrospective look at Dad, and we're beginning to ask questions about the role he played in our current joys and struggles.

For Christian women, a look at how our fathers affected us can have deep and intensely spiritual significance. The God we serve has revealed himself as "Our Father, who art in heaven. . . ." As many of us are discovering, a clearer perspective on our ties without earthly fathers results in a new growth in faith and security in our heavenly Father's love.

For me, this analysis of fathers and daughters has been anything but an exercise. Because of the insights I've uncovered, I've found healing for inner wounds I never expected to escape, and freedom from emotional bondages I've fought against for years. I've come away with a warmth and respect for my father I never imagined I could feel, and a deepening confidence in God that I've longed to experience.

But I'm telling you the end of my journey before you know its start. It all began, you see, with The Dream. . . .

◇ 1 ◇

Did Dad Make a Difference?

T his was a silly time in my life for a nightmare.
I was, after all, a grown woman with children who
needed comfort from their own occasional bad dreams.
And nothing in my life seemed nightmarish. I had a warm,
steady marriage, two great kids who were finally both
potty trained, financial breathing room for the first time in
years, my fifth book safely delivered to the publisher, and
a marvelously uncomplicated life tucked away in a big blue
farmhouse in rural Iowa. This particular year I'd made
peace with my first gray hairs, taken up jogging and even
mastered our personal computer. There was a lot of evidence that should have given me confidence in a sense of
accomplishment.

That's why the intensity and the emotion of what I
came to refer to as The Dream caught me so unprepared.

---

*I am a little girl, perhaps seven or eight, and standing on the
platform of a run-down train station situated in the middle of a
forlorn countryside. A crowd pushes and shoves around me. I feel*

frightened and confused, knowing it is imperative that I board the train, but not knowing where to go. Suddenly the huge black steam-powered locomotive begins to pull away from the station.

I take off after it as it starts up and begins to pick up speed. I am running now as fast as my child-legs can go after that enormous, terrifying engine. The distance between us widens, but I know that I must keep running because I have to catch up or something devastating will happen to me. But as I half run, half stumble down the tracks, the train pulls away. I collapse into a ditch beside the tracks, and huddle there alone in the cold as night falls. I begin to sob in terror and despair . . .

———————

I awoke from The Dream crying. My husband rolled over and sat up.

"Honey, what's wrong?" he mumbled, laying a warm hand on my shoulder.

"I had a dream . . ."

"Can you tell me?"

I tried. But as the fresh sense of a little girl's desolation swept over me, I could only sob. Mike could do nothing but hold me until my tears subsided.

The next morning, settled in our navy wing chairs, with the early morning July sunshine streaming over us and our first cups of coffee in hand, The Dream seemed less paralyzing. We made amateur-psychiatrist stabs at probing the symbolism of missing the train, with no conclusion. Even before our coffee cooled we had given up.

We did agree, however, that whatever it meant, it seemed to point to a well-hidden, but obviously painful inner conflict. Some resolution probably needed to take place, but muddling around in my psyche would have to wait. The green beans needed picking, the quarterly sales tax had to be figured, and the house demanded a good cleaning for weekend guests.

I didn't have time to pursue The Dream the next day, either, or the next. But a month or so later, while at a business conference, it came after me.

Alone in my room one morning, I sat quietly with journal in hand, reviewing the events of the week. I hadn't slept well the night before, and felt the need to do some inner housecleaning. I'd behaved badly in several personal encounters and felt discouraged and condemned. Why did I always try too hard to please? And why did it annihilate me when I thought I'd displeased others? I wrote in my journal:

> *I fear that if I let down my guard enough to be myself, others will know what an inadequate person I am. And if they find out what I'm really like, I'm going to be abandoned. So I have to work harder to cover my weakness and keep up appearances or I'm going to be left alone in the world.*

As I wrote, images from my nightmare came back. It was as if mental tumblers clicked into place, and the door to understanding swung wide. The big black huffing locomotive seemed to represent the way my father lived life—loud, aggressive, strong, headed somewhere important. And not at all in need of me. Like the little girl running down the track, I'd lived afraid that if I didn't try hard and struggle and perform, I'd wind up left behind. Forsaken.

In the year that followed, questions about the relationship between fathers and daughters stalked me. Was there something really so important about this father-daughter business? Up to that point, I'd assumed it was a mother who shaped her daughter's outcome; Dad mattered to boys, and as a provider for girls, but not in many other ways. If he was kind and involved it was a nice bonus, but his involvement was certainly not essential for a girl's growth into secure womanhood. Why would my relationship with my dad affect me so deeply?

In my mind, we were barely connected at all. At our house, Papa was unquestionably the Chief (my mother's title for him), a strong, outspoken, imposing man, and such a natural leader that we used to say of him, "When he comes on the scene, he *is* the scene."

Dad was definitely the kind of man no one could ignore. He started working at our local Veterans Hospital in Knoxville, Iowa, as an aide stuck on the graveyard shift, but by the time he retired he was head of the Protective Section, earning the highest wage-rating possible without a college education. Though he had completed only the tenth grade, he won a seat on the local school board, and made an impact there that people remember to this day. Even now, in his late seventies, he's just been elected president of a Kiwanis Club he joined only a couple of years ago.

I always stood in awe of him. But I thought our day-to-day relationship had been insignificant.

I recall only a handful of times we ever talked personally, and those incidents involved either corrections for petty annoyances ("No singing at the supper table"), or handing down logistical life decisions ("Yes, you can take the car to Omaha"). The only time I ever remember us doing anything alone together was just before my sixteenth birthday, when he attempted a driving lesson. I stopped by his office after school, and when we got into the car to start home, he told me I could drive. So I put the car in reverse, but hadn't backed up ten feet before he corrected me sharply for something that wasn't quite right.

I got teary but, trying not to really cry, got out of the car and walked around to the passenger side. "You drive," I said. He slid over to the wheel, I got in, and we drove home in silence. Neither of us ever mentioned it again.

Looking back now on what I've thought of as "the driving disaster," I see we had no communication bridge.

I did learn to drive (from my mother), and this incident with him faded from my mind. But I went on to womanhood assuming that my lack of personal connection to my father had little effect on me—that is, until my dream showed me differently. At about the same time I discovered that my "insignificant" relationship with my dad was in no way insignificant. It was then I met Dr. Daniel Trobisch, the well-known German-born psychoanalyst who ministers to teenagers in Austria through the Young Life organization. Dr. Trobisch told me of his extensive study of how a woman's relationship with her father has profound effects on her relationship with God. Her father's attitude and behavior, Dr. Trobisch discovered, largely provides the stuff from which a woman develops a strong or weak sense of God-confidence, womanly confidence, and self-confidence.

The combination of my own questions and this professional's insights launched me into a three-year "dig" into the mysteries of the father-daughter relationship. I found that studies by behavioral scientists confirm that girls do grow up differently in accordance with the ways their fathers behave toward them.

Dr. William Appleton, a Boston psychologist, lays it out like this: "If a woman understands her development with respect to her father . . . she'll have enough information to help her in all facets of her life."[1]

Suzanne Fields, in her book *Like Father, Like Daughter,* insists: "Her father's imprint marks a woman's identity for all time—her sense of self, her work, her love relationships, her understanding of the sexual differences. . . . The important qualities of psychological development are strongly influenced by the first man in a woman's life."[2]

---

[1]William Appleton, *Fathers and Daughters* (New York: Doubleday, 1981), xii.
[2]Suzanne Fields, *Like Father, Like Daughter: How Father Shapes the Woman His Daughter Becomes* (Boston: Little, Brown and Company, 1983), 29–30.

Bill Ewing, director of the Black Hills Christian Life Ministries in Rapid City, South Dakota, told me, "I have never seen a female client whose struggles didn't in some way connect to deficits in the care she received from her father."

Dr. Trobisch, in his study of German women, concluded that only about 15 percent of the women he interviewed grew up enjoying effective fathering. If his sample transfers to American women—and my personal research among women leads me to believe it does—then more than eight out of every ten women feel some pangs of "father hunger."

The reason a woman has this need—or *capacity*—to receive inner strength from a father is simple to understand. A woman's relationship with her father was designed by God as a springboard to finding peace with herself, with men, and with her heavenly Father. Psychology confirms this. As Appleton says, "The more a woman understands her father's effect and makes use of this knowledge, the more she will be able to enjoy her husband . . . sexually, emotionally, and intellectually, the freer she will be to pursue and advance in her career, the better she will be as a mother to her own children, and the richer her life will become."[3]

Dad isn't the only factor influencing who we are as women; our mothers played a large part, of course. My mother, for instance, played the role of go-between, shielding us from what she perceived as a sometimes too-gruff daddy.

There were other influences in our lives, too. Other family members, teachers, coaches, and a host of others all made a difference in each one of us. In my case, I was the fifth of six children, following in the shadow of four

---

[3]Appleton, 1.

older brothers, each, it appeared to me, as loud and sure and dynamic and hard-to-get-close-to as my father.

Not only did these family scenarios in which we grew up "shape" us, but *we* played a part in how those inter-actions developed as well. Children, after all, are not inert lumps of wet clay, passively punched and poked into shape by people and events around them. We helped de-termine our directions by how we responded to the people in our lives.

Though our fathers aren't the only determining influ-ence in our lives, it is true that their impact may be the *most ignored.* And because we haven't given this most im-portant relationship its due, it's possible that women over-look a major resource for moving along toward maturity.

In the five years since "The Dream," I've made some liberating discoveries:

1. My father did play a major part in shaping the woman I've become—in relation to men, to other women, to myself, and to God.

2. Understanding and admitting the extent of his effect on me has been both joyful and painful.

3. Facing the effects of this relationship honestly has unbound me to grow in faith and confidence. Jesus said, "The truth shall make you free" (John 8:32). I now see the potential for deeper emotional bonding with God, more balanced relationships with both men and women, and greater confidence in my own worth.

I believe these same things can happen for every woman who begins her own journey toward dealing with the dad of her past.

So, Where Do We Begin?

It starts, of course, with taking time to truthfully look at your own dad and his effectiveness as a father. But what do we mean by effective fathering? Is it simply "bread-winning," as we thought twenty years ago? Or does it have to include changing diapers, getting up with sick children, being involved with teenaged heartaches and college traumas?

I believe there's a simple and authoritative way to evaluate fathering, because Scripture says it is from *God* that "all fatherhood, earthly or heavenly, derives its name" (Ephesians 4:13, Phillips). From God's instructions to fathers we can get a true and balanced picture of the ingredients of effective fathering. Though these ingredients are taught throughout Scripture, they're summarized well in one statement:

> Fathers, provoke not your children to wrath: but bring them up in the nurture and admonition of the Lord. (Ephesians 6:4)

This powerful instruction actually contains four different ways in which a father is to influence his daughter's life.

First, he is *to bring her up*—that is, to actively involve himself in her life.

Second, he is to *nurture her.* Nurture speaks of *warmth* that is expressed in healthy, wholesome words and in respectful physical touch.

Third, he is to *admonish her,* and that means he is to see that she is well-taught and well-disciplined.

And last, he is to *let her go,* toward the Lord. He is not to keep her as his possession forever, but to launch her into her own life under the Fatherhood of God.

Involvement means being there for his daughter. *Warmth* and *discipline* mean being there in the right way. And *launching* means letting go when the time is right. When her dad supplies each of these ingredients as God intended, he provides a setting in which his daughter can grow toward wholeness and toward the Lord. But fathering gone awry can produce dismal effects in a daughter's life.

To me, the journey of growth begins by understanding the four greatest "hungers" that God built into each one of us—the hunger for involvement, warmth, discipline and the need for launching. It requires a look back and honest assessment of the dad of our past. It means coming to terms with who he really was, and who he wasn't, when we are able to look at him minus the colorations of time and our own ideals. For some, it may well mean grieving for what never was in order to come out on the other side, free of the hungers that drive us to unhealthy, immature habits of living. And finally, we are ready to begin embracing, and to be embraced by the One perfect Father who is always there.[4]

---

[4]The names and identifying details of the women written about in this book are purposely fictitious to protect the privacy of those who graciously shared their experiences with me.

◇ 2 ◇

The Hunger for Involvement

The singing/songwriting couple, Steve and Annie Chapman, whose music centers on home and family themes, perform one song called "Her Daddy's Love." Some of the deeply moving lyrics say things like, "There's a place in her heart that can only be filled with her daddy's love." And "If your little girl grows up without daddy's love, she may feel empty. . . ."

These words stir up a hunger. But what exactly are daughters hungry for? I believe it's the four aspects of fathering we've just discovered in Scripture: *involvement, warmth, discipline* and *launching.* How dads do or don't deliver on these four facets of fathering will shape the adult women their daughters become.

Involvement: "Please Be There for Me"

In His instructions to the children of Israel as they readied themselves to take the Promised Land, God said this:

These commandments that I give you today are to be upon your hearts. Impress them on your children. Talk about them when you sit at home and when you walk along the road, when you lie down and when you get up. (Deuteronomy 6:6, 7)

The father who fulfilled this instruction had to be an involved parent. No absentee father can instruct his children as they relax at home, and as they take walks together, and when he tucks them in, and when they sit down to breakfast together.

How Involved Was Your Father?

Your father may have left through death or divorce, and therefore wasn't involved at all. Or your dad may have been around every single day, but never connected with you emotionally. Even though he was "there," he wasn't. Such was Darlene's experience.

As she describes it: "My dad had a steady eight-to-five job all his life. When he wasn't at his work, he was home. We lived on a farm, and he worked the land to generate a second income, so about the only time he wasn't around was when he left for his work in town."

Yet, when Darlene struggles to recall her father's parenting skills, she hesitates. "I can't tell you whether my father treated me harshly or warmly, because he left almost all interactions with me up to my mother. I guess the truth is, even though we lived in the same house, he was barely involved with me at all."

Dr. Roland Fleck and his colleagues from Rosemead School of Psychology studied 160 college women whose fathers lived at home at least until their daughters were thirteen years of age. They looked at the quality of each father-daughter relationship, then at each woman's ability to adjust to life.[1]

---

[1] The women's sexual activity, anxiety level, and identification with a female role were tested. See J. Roland Fleck, et al., "Father Psychological Absence and Heterosexual Behavior, Personal Adjustment and Sex-Typing in Adolescent Girls," *Adolescence*, Vol. XV, No. 60, Winter 1980, 847–859.

These researchers found that girls with "psychologically absent" fathers showed many of the same difficulties with life and men as did girls whose fathers virtually disappeared after a divorce. Simply having her dad living at home isn't enough to assure a daughter's healthy development. What matters is how much he was involved *emotionally* with her.

What do we mean by involvement? How does it form the basis for the father-daughter relationship? On the most basic level, involvement means communication. If Dad is not involved, there can be no communication, and therefore no positive expression of warmth or discipline. In the end, an uninvolved father can never launch his daughter into adulthood because he was never connected to her inner needs in the first place. She may leave home for a job or marriage or college, but within her, the uncared-for little girl is chained to a lifetime of searching for a strong figure who will fill the void inside her, the kind of deep affirmation that gives the confidence we all need to cope with the difficulties and unsureties of the adult world.

Not only does the daddy void affect her inner life, it will profoundly affect her relationships with other men— her judgments and expectations, her longing-for and intimidation by them. It will push her to a constant, though not always conscious, search for *something*. But what?

Distant Dads: Searching Daughters

E. Mavis Hetherington, a researcher from the University of Virginia, set out to discover how a woman's life-development is affected when her father isn't there. Her landmark study, in which she compared girls who'd lost their fathers through divorce or death with father-present girls, produced a profile of daughters on a search. Though they went about this search in different ways, the daughters of divorcees and widows presented a portrait of in-completeness and longing that affected how they related to men, to themselves, and to their work. Though Dr. Hetherington's subjects were teenagers, many adult women with distant dads identify with her study. The forms our searching takes may be less flamboyant than our teenaged counterparts, but the *patterns* still hold true.

———

What does a woman with a distant dad search for?

First, she is often searching for a deeply satisfying re-lationship with the man or men in her life. Ideally, a father should offer to his young daughter a wonderful, warm place of refuge where she can learn to love and be loved by a man without all the complexities of erotic impulses that will later color her male-female relationships. He pro-vides for his little girl what one author calls an "oasis," where she can be adored by a wonderful man for no rea-son other than that she exists. In the safety of this oasis she can learn from a man, work out conflicts with a man, and develop the skills of innocent flirtation that will serve her later when the object of her affection is a man of her own.

But what if there was no safe "oasis"? What if Dad was more like a desert mirage, there in appearance only? Then chances are she will be less likely to trust in the love and security offered by any man. She may live with a vague, nameless anxiety that one day the bottom will fall out—that the man she cares about will lose interest in her, fail to support her, or that he will simply not be there when she desperately needs him most. Just like Dad.

Without any day-to-day life experiences of interacting with a man, these women have fewer skills in loving or fighting or growing with a real man. Instead of a life part-ner, they may subconsciously look for a man who will be a daddy to a little girl. Along with all the regular husbanding functions, this man they seek must also protect them and shelter them and coddle them and dote on them in the way only a fantasy father could. The place where this "you-need-to-be-my-daddy" confusion may cause the biggest problems is in the bedroom.

It may even happen that these daughters settle for less than what they could in a man. Without a caring father to appreciate, a girl might be more susceptible to hollow generalizations: "Men are no good"; "You can't count on a man to be there when you need him." Not expecting any better behavior from the men she encounters, she may be too quick to commit herself to an unworthy man, simply because she doesn't believe a better man can be found.

And then some women take an altogether different approach. Some take their "daddy-must-have-been-perfect" attitude and transfer it to all men. Consequently, she believes all men are far superior to her so she always needs to defer to them and certainly to feel inferior around them. This woman makes a dream partner for an extremely insecure man who seeks worship from his wife rather than love. Though they may have few conflicts in their early period together, years of living with the reality of this man, combined with her growing maturity, usually force the "inferior" wife to remove her rose-colored glasses. Superman isn't always super, she discovers, and trouble erupts.

Second, the daughter of an uninvolved father may suffer from a search to find a meaningful life's contribution. She may be quite devoid of an overall life plan to guide her.

Dr. Hetherington noted that daughters of both widows and divorcees showed more "instrumental" dependency on women—that is, they asked for more help from women in doing tasks than did the father-present girls.

This dependence on women (perhaps fed also by a distrust of men) may lead these father-absent daughters into an all-female world of work. A woman may excel in the steno pool where her supervisor is Ms. Somebody-or-Other, but a promotion to administrative assistant to Mr. Whomever may leave her frustrated and frightened. As long as the girls in Dr. Hetherington's study were being interviewed by a woman, all three groups of girls seemed equally comfortable. But when a man asked the questions, both groups of father-absent girls showed signs of considerable anxiety—nail biting, hair, lip and finger pulling, plucking at their clothes.

Transfer this anxiety to a work situation, and it's not surprising that a father-absent woman is more likely to complain that she doesn't "feel comfortable" in a male-supervised job.

On the other end of the spectrum, some girls deprived of fathers become super-achievers in the world of work. This attitude produces a sense of pseudo-independence. It's a chip-on-the-shoulder sort of "I'm going to prove I can match you—with no help from anyone!" This woman works harder, longer and better to do what she sets out to do. Work becomes a competition to be won or lost, rather than a source of fulfillment in itself. She is wary of dependency, and so professional success, no matter the cost, provides a guarantee of *in*dependence. This pseudo-independence can mask a fear of intimacy. Small children who fear closeness can become hyperactive sideliners, or else too grown-up. Both are defenses to push people away from seeing what's inside them. Adults can use the same defenses. If a woman never needs a man again, she can never be abandoned again, as she once was.

Of course, not every woman who is successful in the work force is out there plugging because she's trying to best men. Nor is every homemaker a wounded daughter, hiding in her split-level dollhouse trying desperately to remain a little girl. But if a woman's life choices are not satisfying—yet she feels no freedom to make changes—it might be worthwhile to ask herself how she got to the place she is.

———

Third, a father-absent daughter can have real trouble finding a comfortable distance from Mom.

Dr. Hetherington probed the mothers of her father-absent daughters and found that both widows and divorcees reported being overprotective of their daughters. Perhaps father-absent girls struggle more with Mom over their independence because they have further to go in winning it than do other girls.

Sometimes fatherless girls fight with Mom because they're so much more dependent on her and they're angry that they are. With Daddy's love gone, losing Mom would mean losing all hope of parental affection, so a daughter can't afford to risk losing her love. But a daughter may resent this feeling of not having an option. At a time in her life when growing independence means emotional survival, she knows she can't risk too much independence because if she loses Mom, she's lost it all.

Another factor may be at work in the fracas between mothers and their father-absent daughters. A daughter may be furious at her dad for not being there for her, but since he's not there to be mad at, she may transfer her anger to the only one around: Mom.

Jo Ann was warned by her physician to expect this reaction from her teenage daughter after Jo Ann's husband left home for a younger woman. At the time, it seemed unlikely, because Jo Ann was as close to model motherhood as anyone you've seen. She had unselfishly provided

stability and security and involvement for the children during the years her husband went here and there, changing
jobs, trying to become someone important. Surely there
would be no cause for her daughters to be angry at their
mother.

But one day her daughter exploded: "If you'd treated
him better, he wouldn't have left!"

Of course, all the blaming and rebellion and ugliness
had little to do with Jo Ann's deficits as a mother. Her
daughter seethed with anger at her dad's desertion, but to
be angry with him might mean losing even the measly,
few weekends she spent with him. Instead she chose the
only "safe" place to vent her rage—at her accepting, loving
mom.

How many women carry around anger toward their
mothers? How much of it is really misplaced rage at a dad
who was never there when needed?

———

It is complex, indeed, this need we daughters have for
Dad to be a part of our deeper lives. If he wasn't, we can
pay the price through all our woman years in a hundred
different ways. And yet there is tremendous hope for freedom and maturity, as we will see in later chapters. We
need not live our lives with the wrong belief that God is,
like an earthly dad, uncaring, unwilling to protect us, unwilling to guide and direct us into meaningful lives.
Though men (or women) may abandon us, God does not!

An unfulfilled hunger for involvement generates one
set of struggles. The hunger for warmth leads to yet another, which we will now explore.

◊ **3** ◊

The Hunger for Warmth

Kristy's father carried the load of child-care for his two daughters from the time they were born. When the girls were in elementary school, Dad was the one who rousted them out of bed in the morning and saw them safely off to school. The girls' teachers called him, not his wife, for conferences. He decided about summer camps, and saw to it his daughters cleaned their rooms. Definitely an involved father.

But his involvement showed itself only in strong discipline. The rules were clear—and plentiful. Threats abounded, punishments were swift. Anything less than a straight-A report card meant grounding for a month—and that was when Kristy was only a third grader!

As Kristy grew up, the part of God's nature she had the most trouble connecting with was His warmth. She'd hear ministers speak of God's affection for His children, and read scriptures like Hosea 11:1, 4, "When Israel was a child, I loved him. . . . I led them with cords of human kindness, and ties of love." But Kristy could never feel a sense of reality in the words.

Kristy's experience points to a second fathering hunger in women: the hunger for warmth.

"I Accept You"

By his warmth a father tells his daughter, "You are acceptable to me. I like who you are."

Warmth is *love*. A loving father communicates affection in nonsexual *touching*: being cuddled on Daddy's lap; a hug around the shoulders; a pat on the back; a squeeze on her hand.

Warmth is *praise*. The wise father praises his daughter for both her femininity and her achievements. Girls who only receive affirmation for their sweetness and cuteness can grow up to be little dolls, too weak to make it in the real world where merely being cute and coy won't pay the electric bill. And girls who are only praised for their achievements can struggle to develop a deeply settled sense of their own femininity.

Warmth is *acceptance*. It is a father letting his daughter know, "You are different from me. Not only are you a different personality, but you are female. And because you are different, you have much to teach me. You don't have to be exactly like me to be okay."

What happens to a daughter when her father can't be pleased? She becomes driven by a hunger for praise, warmth and acceptance. A girl raised without warmth from her dad grows up driven to protect herself from rejection. Going into life with such formidable burdens as these takes a toll on a woman's relationships, on her performance, and on her sexual identity.

The Driven Daughter and Her Relationships

Wouldn't it be safe to assume that a woman whose father rarely expressed warmth would be drawn to a man with all the qualities she so longed for from her father? Doesn't it seem reasonable she'd marry someone warm and tender, expressive and kind?

Logical, perhaps, but often that's not what happens. Statistics show, for instance, that girls with alcoholic fathers very often marry alcoholics or compulsives, thus jumping right back onto the same disastrous emotional merry-go-round on which they grew up. Women with unpleasable fathers seem doomed to a fascination with the same kind of people. Why?

When a woman is drawn to an *overbearing man,* she may at first love his drive, his decisiveness, his ambition. It troubles her little that it's always her plans they change in deference to his. She brushes aside the fact that the time they spent the night before in "deep conversation" was mostly two hours of his views and feelings. Somehow she doesn't notice that he asked her little about her thoughts, and didn't care to pursue them when offered. She may tend to think, "He's smarter than I am about most things, anyway."

But when they marry, and their years together increase, she begins to describe him differently. She uses phrases like "selfish," "always wants to do it his way," "doesn't listen to what I say," "won't support me in anything I want to do."

This overbearing man is a duplicate of her unpleasable father. That is, in fact, the reason she married him, though she doesn't know it. She'll pay nearly any price to get him and keep him because he offers something very valuable to her. Life with him is a theater where she can replay the male rejection she felt in her childhood, with hopes that this time she'll be able to change things and win *this* man's warmth and love.

One woman I know chose not only an overbearing husband but also overbearing female friends. The women who fascinated her most were hard-driving, super-successes who loved to hear how wonderful they were, and loved to try to help her become more like them.

Driven women can also be attracted to *troubled men*. Why? Because the turmoil these men create feels normal. Thus, many daughters of alcoholics marry into the same problem all over again. Fortunately or unfortunately, humans can somehow survive in almost any life situation. When a daughter has been consistently shoved away by her father, acceptance may make her feel uneasy—guilty perhaps, or overwhelmingly unworthy, or under pressure to keep her performance up to a level that she feels will merit the acceptance she's receiving. To this woman, coldness, harshness, or chaos may actually feel more comfortable than loving stability.

Her troubled man may also be a *passive man*. Women in these relationships often say, "I was attracted to him because I knew that with just a little help from me, he could change for the better." These women can be particularly susceptible to the plaintive cry from a married man who says his wife doesn't understand him. Or to listen sympathetically to the justifications of a man who's failed professionally when he says he never got a fair shake from his employers. She can control the passive man, or even the needy man, and that is what makes him so attractive.

She may disguise the control, even to herself, by labeling it "helping." But while she is helping him get the career he deserves, or helping him take off a few pounds, or helping him learn to share his feelings, the relationship stays on her turf. She stays in control.

Sometimes, an odd thing happens to a relationship like this when the man is forced to change, for one reason or another. Though she may claim she wishes he were more dynamic, or successful, or helpful with the children, a woman may subtly undermine her husband's efforts at assertion by becoming unpleasable herself. It's not uncommon for a drunk's wife to leave him once he gives up the bottle. One such woman said, "It was as hard for me to give up my addiction to an unbalanced relationship as it was for him to give up booze."

To a woman who has never won warmth from her father, emotionally healthy men can generate one of two responses: they bore her, or they frighten her. She may describe a healthy man as, "Well, nice . . . okay, I guess. But there's no electricity there. He just doesn't captivate me." He doesn't, because there's no sweet promise of duplicating Daddy's unpleasable nature, which would give her another opportunity to try to win him (or his stand-in). The first man in her life was not pleased with her. She feels on a subconscious level that his verdict was the right one: She is hopelessly flawed. So any subsequent man who accepts her must not be worth much. He must not have taste, or he'd know at once she wasn't acceptable.

A man who offers her warmth and acceptance has two strikes against him before he gets up to bat. The challenge to "attain the unattainable" charges up the electricity in her relationships. With a healthy man, the generator never kicks in because he accepts her for who she is. And healthy men offer the intimacy she says she longs for, but when it comes, it frightens her away. With intimacy comes the challenge of honesty and mature interdependence.

Melissa said, "I never understood how much my father's harshness affected me until I took one of those little tests women's magazines always run about your love life. One of the questions asked was 'Are the men you are attracted to usually attracted to you?' The answer for me was no. As I thought about it, I realized that as far back as high school, the boys I liked never liked me. I did have dates and boyfriends, but not with the boys I really wanted to win over. Now that I have better perspective on how my dad's lack of affection hurt me, I see I was attracted to those boys *because* they didn't like me. Their disinterest made them prizes worth going after. Of course I like being liked by nearly any male, but those elusive, hard-to-please types kept me fascinated long after I'd lost interest in the guys who were steadier, more accepting."

The unpleasable father prepares his daughter for a lifetime of struggles with men—struggles to connect with them, then struggles to find satisfaction with the one she marries.

The Driven Daughter and Her Performance

Most commonly, whatever a driven daughter does, she is driven to seek *perfection*. Dr. John Musser, a clinical psychologist in private practice in California, reports that he deals with a significant number of women like this. "They tend to be very high achievers," he reflects, "but never satisfied with their own performance, often because they've never been *enough* for their fathers." Driven achievers never "arrive" in their own thinking. Therefore, they can never rest.

Some perfectionists disguise themselves well. Do you have a friend whose desk or kitchen is always a huge mess of disorder? Though she'd laugh at the idea, she may be a perfectionist in disguise. Such people get tired of trying to reach their own unreachable expectations. Instead of settling for less, they simply give up. Such is the plight of the *frustrated perfectionist*. To a perfectionist, life must be black or white. No gray. Ever. She's the best or the worst; a winner or a loser. Therefore, if her house can't always be perfect, she quits trying, and perhaps directs her energies into other arenas where it is possible to control life and meet her out-of-sight expectations.

Either way, an unpleasable father can produce a daughter driven to perfection. And when her inner voice can never say she's done well, her self-esteem can go nowhere but down.

In one study, college women were asked to name the color of ink in which certain words were written. To make the test more difficult, each of the words was the name of a color other than the color ink it was written in. Every time a woman gave an incorrect answer, the experimenter called out "wrong," and she had her correct herself. This put the women under a degree of stress. The group of women who did most poorly on the test were those whose fathers had been high in their demands, but negligent in expressing love.

There may be another kind of effect on a woman's performance when she has an unpleasant father: She may never develop creatively simply because she's *afraid to try*.

Dana had loved science ever since high school, and her stint as a volunteer in a local hospital was one of the most rewarding experiences of her teen years. So when her own children were older and an opportunity opened up to start a nursing program, everyone who knew her thought she'd jump at the chance.

But within a few months, she'd dropped her classes. "It's my husband's fault," she told everyone. "He wouldn't support me." The truth was, he had made some minor complaints one evening about how much better meals used to be before Dana became a student. But Dana *heard* in his remark something he never intended: "I do not want you to become a nurse!" Within two weeks, she quit school because she took his remark as rejection.

Is Dana overly sensitive? Overly dependent on his hand-holding? Perhaps. But when you know that her stepfather never supported her in anything she did, her lack of confidence makes more sense. Now, ten years after quitting nurses training, Dana still hasn't found a job to fit her—but it's largely because she's afraid to try and then to stick with any venture until she reaches proficiency.

The Driven Daughter and Her Sexuality

Researcher Allen Gerson surveyed highly promiscuous women and asked them to identify characteristics of their fathers. These women chose the words: forceful, hateful, unlikable, distant, and threatening.

Without fatherly affection, a girl comes to believe that her hunger for touch can only be satisfied in one context, that of sexual encounters. This hunger for nonsexual touching never received from their father gnaws at many women. It can get them trapped in marriages and sexual relationships they never really wanted.

In interviews with nearly 100 women who had three or more unwanted pregnancies, Dr. Marc Hollender, a noted psychiatrist, found that nearly all the women said they had never been meaningfully touched by their fathers. They believed that sexual activity was the price that must be paid for what they really wanted, to be cuddled and held.

But for women who do not choose promiscuity, a lack of warmth from their fathers can give girls a bent for escape into mental infidelity—indulging in fantasy relationships that if acted out would be wrong. In a classic work on fathers and daughters, Marjorie Leonard, a professor of psychiatry, concluded: "Whenever a father fails to participate (in the girl's upbringing), she responds by providing herself with a fantasized relationship to an image of her father."[1] To the adult woman, these fantasies may take the form of imagined romantic encounters, not with her

---

[1]Leonard, Marjorie R., "Fathers and Daughters," (*International Journal of Psychoanalysis*, 1966) p. 329.

father, but with men she knows who are like him.

Until change is unleashed in her life, the driven daughter will live her whole life with an unhappy legacy passed on from a dad who couldn't give warmth. She is driven to seek out acceptance in relationships, yet making foolish choices of those she tries to be close to. Driven to perfection in her work or home, but seeing even her successes as not good enough. Driven to sexual dissatisfaction, yet longing for real love. But then, the Father whom we will meet shortly is One who not only approves, He changes, strengthens and empowers. He is the Father who *is* love.

◇ **4** ◇

The Hunger for Discipline

One young woman who was asked about her father's part in disciplining her said, "The first thing I think of is the time I stole some marking pens from a local store.

"Dad made me go back and confess what I'd done. I was nine at the time, and I knew I'd die from humiliation. I cried all the way to the store and all the way home, but my dad didn't just send me to do it—he went with me.

"Afterward, he held me on his lap and talked about courage and integrity. I don't remember the whole speech, but I do remember that I knew he was proud of me for setting things right.

"It's funny," she commented, "how a negative incident like that could be such a strong part of the bond I feel now between us."

Her account makes an important point: Love and guidance go hand-in-hand. Warmth without guidance and discipline is not real love—it is, at best, indulgence; at worst, it is consigning a child to the uncertainties of an undirected life. That's why the book of Proverbs so firmly instructs, "Discipline your son, and he will give you peace; he will bring delight to your soul" (Proverbs 29:17). Of course, this admonition holds true for daughters as well.

Please Teach Me to Control Myself

Psychologist John Musser studied college women to see what effect their fathers' discipline or guidance (Musser used the term "control") had on their daughters' lives. He concluded that the more a father disciplined his daughter—coupling discipline with acceptance and love—the higher her self-esteem, self-reliance, assertiveness, contentment, and self-control.[1]

A father's discipline gives a daughter the security of limits—but it gives her something more as well. Psychologist Henry Biller admonished fathers: "Your kind of love—more judging and more challenging—is vital to the child. *You dare more with the child* [emphasis mine], you help (her) to push (herself) and to use (her) talents to their fullest."[2]

A strong father's leadership, guidance and discipline give a daughter a sense of mature, directed daring, along with the capacity for focused effort toward a goal. And conversely, it is this directed daring that the daughter of a passive, non-disciplining father lacks. No wonder daughters of passive fathers often become undirected, undisciplined, or domineering.

The weak father can be difficult to discriminate from the distant dad. But one difference in the two stands out. The undisciplining father was *there* when you were growing up, though he exercised little control in your household. Of course the simplest clue to a too-weak father

[1]John M. Musser, Ph.D. and J. Roland Fleck, Ed.D., "The Relationship of Paternal Acceptance and Control to College Females' Personality Adjustment," (*Adolescence,* Vol. XVII, No. 72, Winter 1983), 907–916.
[2]Henry Biller and David Meredith, *Father Power* (New York: David McKay Co., 1974), 8.

comes when a woman growls that her most troublesome parent was her mother, not her father. One such daughter was asked what message she would send to her father if she could. "Easy," she smiled. "I'd tell him, 'Dad, thanks for being nice to me, but you should have sent Mom to a psychiatrist!' "

When we discuss a father's leadership in the home and his part in guiding his daughter, we're not pushing for an all-powerful patriarch who feels called to keep the little woman and all the kids doing his bidding. Nor are we proposing that a dad's leadership in his daughter's life exclude her mother's influence. Balance is certainly called for. Henry Biller offers wise advice to fathers on this point:

"There is not a 'power see-saw' in the family. If you become more effective with your children, it doesn't mean your wife will become less so. In fact, using father power will aid your wife in becoming a more effective parent. It could relieve her of the enormous burden of child-rearing she has had to assume because of the widespread noninvolvement of the father in the family."[3]

The need for a Dad-Mom-child link is not just some traditionalists' fantasy, hearkening back to the days of yesteryear. Psychology confirms what the Bible has taught all along—that God ordained the father to be an important voice in a child's life for establishing strength and character at the bedrock level of a child's soul.

The mother-child connection begins nine months before the baby sees the light of day. It was Mother's heartbeat and her voice the baby heard during those months within her body. It is Mother's life rhythms that set the stage for the baby's own rhythm. This mother-child bonding is beautiful and necessary for the child to thrive. But for this child to grow into a full maturity, this bond must be opened to include others.

---

[3]Biller, p. 7.

In most cases, her rescuer from the exclusivity of Mother's arms is Dad. He is the first Important Other outside this mother-daughter connection and he, by his very maleness, represents a world outside. Dad is bigger, his voice deeper, his face rougher, his cradling different. If from infancy, the twosome can open to a threesome, the little girl has a good chance to go into life securely rooted and ready to branch out. One authority describes this process as prying the child loose from her mother-dependency.

But when Dad does not find a place in the mother-daughter union—as can be the case when a father is never involved in discipline—Mom becomes both mother and father and, therefore, is often unable to do either job well. Providing discipline for a daughter isn't a task categorically assigned to one parent or the other, but if a father takes no initiative in providing direction and discipline in the family, his daughter will pay for his neglect all through her adult life.

Let's consider some of the possible effects.

A Passion for Passive Men or Overbearing Men

When her father is uninvolved in guidance and discipline, a woman can be drawn either to a passive man she can control, or to an overbearing man who she hopes will be strong enough to rescue her from the dominion of her mother.

Ruler of a Passive Husband

Ann chose a passive man. Gentle, sweet, agreeable, moldable. He makes the money. She decides how it will be spent. When she spends more than he makes, he works longer to make more. She plans his free time, what magazines he subscribes to, who his confidants will be. In his off hours, she schedules her activities, knowing he'll be there to keep the kids. He goes for weeks without sex because she isn't in the mood, and her mood is *the* determinant. Ann makes all the policy decisions concerning the children, and supervises him as he carries out her rules.

Even with all this control, however, Ann is unhappy. Her husband often fixes dinner while she's off seeing her psychiatrist.

"Victim" of an Overbearing Husband

Adrian chose an overbearing husband. "Jon was the first person ever to tell my mother to shut up," she says. "Secretly, I loved it." Adrian needed his strength to cut the psychological umbilical cords that bound her to her controlling mother.

This particular combination, "the helpless woman and the rescuer," make for short-range bliss and long-range dissatisfaction. Now, five years after the wedding, Adrian complains that Jon never listens to her, and he runs their home with the same unyielding authority he used to lead a company in Viet Nam. Unfortunately, tyrant-slayers are often tyrants themselves, so women like Adrian who marry a Macho Man in an attempt to escape Mom's domination wind up back under domination of a different sort.

How much better if Adrian's dad had been a true father, strong enough to lead his family in love and wisdom. He would have provided the buffer Adrian and her possessive mother lacked, helping his wife and daughter to love and live with each other, rather than daily battling it out in an on-going power struggle. Then Adrian would have been more ready for a true partnership in marriage, instead of opting for the strong Daddy figure Jon provided.

Women who grew up in a more balanced home, one where Dad played a healthy leadership role, are less likely to stay "victimized" by an overbearing husband. They tend to seek help and counseling for what they recognize as an unhealthy situation for them and their children. This is less true for the adult daughter of a passive father, who is likely to feel that her situation is "normal," even when others tell her it is off-balance.

A passive father affects much more than his daughter's choice of men. His unhappy legacy to her can include unfulfilled potential, unfounded fears and unawakened femaleness.

Unfulfilled Potential

A passive father leaves his daughter devoid of a clear picture of how she fits into the bigger world outside her home. She doesn't understand how the world works, nor how to find a place for herself in it. Psychologist Daniel Trobisch calls this void "a lack of orientation to the world."

Kara was like that. "I wish my dad had helped me grow up," she laments softly. "I have so much trouble thinking beyond the immediate, setting long-range goals, looking at life more objectively. Dad never had a say at home. Because of that, I think, I lack the benefit of a masculine perspective on life. It was more like having two mothers to coddle me along."

In her work on parental dominance, Mavis Hetherington found that a girl from a father-led home not only liked being female, but was also observed by others to have personality traits of both her mother and father—in general, a more balanced personality. Girls from mother-dominated homes were more like their mothers only.

These days, any child who grows up imitating the characteristics of only one of his parents is at a distinct disadvantage. Boys who have never learned to emulate their mother's capacity for tenderness and nurturing are often handicapped in relational skills. And girls who lack a strong identity with their fathers can be prone to quit too quickly, become offended too easily, or offer their ideas too timidly. The net result can be a short-circuiting of their attempts at achievement.

Women with passive fathers also make prime candidates for two "syndromes": the "super-mother syndrome" and the "anti-mothering syndrome." "Super-mothers" work too hard, clean too much, push the kids too insistently to succeed. Anti-mothers—those who bore the brunt of a domineering mother—are the ones who shun mothering all together. "I'll never do to a child what my mother did to me," they assert. And the alternative of a shared parenting experience does not compute. Either way, an undisciplining father leaves his daughter ill-prepared to work in the world, and ill-prepared to mother.

Unfounded Fears

Father is the strong one, the protector, the one who looms as a wall of strength. A woman with a passive father is more likely to grow up with deep-seated insecurities. She senses there's no place of safety from the worst of the world.

The combination of Carol's pushiness and her fearfulness alienate many of those around her. She's chronically afraid. A dizzy spell makes her wonder if she's having a heart attack. Her husband's purchase of a lawn mower without consulting her makes her quake that they're going to overspend and wind up broke. Her fears are depressing enough, but she's so willful that simple, factual reassurances won't diminish her concerns. She refuses to be comforted so easily.

Carol's case is extreme, of course, but women like her who grow up without ever seeing strength or leadership from their father often fail to form a deep, inner sense of feeling cared for and protected. One psychoanalyst, whose patient described having a weak father, quoted the patient as saying, "I get to feeling bad—that things will start to slide. It's a feeling like the house will begin to fall apart or something." *A father without strength leaves his child with a vague sense of impending deterioration.* Something bad is going to happen, and there is no way and no one to stop it.

Unawakened Femaleness

Maybe the saddest legacy a passive father passes to his daughter rests in what he *doesn't* give her. Women with jellyfish for fathers rarely come to a deep and settled confidence in their own *femaleness* because there's been no *maleness* with which to contrast it.

Jewish philosopher Martin Buber speaks of the "dialogical principle"—meaning that in order to discover all the depths of my personality, there has to be a You who calls those depths out of me.

This principle functions when it comes to accepting our sexuality, too. God said, "It is not good for man to be alone." So He created Woman—not an animal, not another man, but Woman—a person different from Man. There is a level on which a woman cannot embrace her femaleness until she sees it in contrast to true maleness.

A woman's relationship with her father should be the incubating place and proving ground for a woman's sense of her own femininity. In this unearned, nonsexual, and therefore totally safe relationship, she should have freedom to be affirmed as a woman. She should know she is different from a man, and that she can merit respect for those differences. She should experience approval and affirmation from a man. She should learn to confront and disagree with a man, express her opinions without apology, accept correction without dissolving. A woman with a passive father, however, experiences little of this "calling out" of the full capacity of her womanhood.

And it is to the inner hunger for launching that we will now turn.

◊ 5 ◊

The Hunger for Launching

Solomon, in Psalm 127:4, described a man's children as "arrows in the hands of a warrior." Arrows are not meant to be carried or displayed in a trophy case. A warrior is successful as he accurately *launches* his arrows. Likewise, a father shines when he equips his daughter to go into life without him. God intended that a father prepare his daughter for life in a world in which Dad is not the only authority. Though one child-rearing authority terms it letting go, I prefer to think of it as launching.

A properly prepared daughter is the one who can enter the adult world unencumbered by a stifling expectancy she must always be rescued from life's troubles and crises by "Daddy" or some daddy-surrogate. She may enjoy Dad's counsel all her life, but still she has grown from a childish dependence, not into independence, but rather into a healthy *interdependence* upon many others in her life.

Please Help Me Stand on My Own

Women like Daphne show signs of a daughter whose father couldn't let her go.

Daphne can't come up with enough praise for her father. Her slim face glows as she recalls how he took her golfing with his friends, then boasted proudly when she brought in more birdies than anyone. She tells about how he taught her carpentry and how to buy insurance, and about how he resisted her adolescent tirades against his strictness. She beams when she remembers how he alone stood by her when she decided to join the army instead of going to college as everyone expected her to.

But her expression clouds when the conversation moves on to her husband. If only he'd listen to her . . . like her dad does. If only he'd find a different job . . . so they could move closer to her dad.

Like Daphne's dad, a father can be involved with his daughter through a good mix of warmth and discipline, yet drop the ball when it comes time to launch her into a mature life of her own. Then a daughter becomes a woman who always knows she can come back to Daddy if the going gets rough, and his reassurance and sympathy and checkbook will make everything all right.

Unfortunately, nowhere else in the world is she able to experience such total giving from one who, on the surface at least, asks nothing back but her appreciation and affection. Like a drug addict, she can be hooked on Dad and emotionally have difficulty in leaving him for an adult life.

And it is possible that he is overly dependent upon her, too. Perhaps that's one reason why he constantly—whether subtly or overtly—encourages her dependence upon him, even when it's in her best interest to learn how to stand without him. He so enjoys his role as Mr. Wonderful in his daughter's eyes that he cannot bear to part with her. He binds her to him by meeting so many of her needs that no one else can match him.

The Daughter Who Is Loved Too Much

Here we are not talking about an incestuous or emotionally abusive relationship (though too many women do suffer from sick treatment at the hands of males in their families). Sexual abuse is not a characteristic of the too-wonderful father.

The problem created by this father is that the "I'll-take-care-of-you-honey" spirit he implants in his daughter hangs on well after his little girl has become a woman. Therefore, the daughter of this kind of father may not be prepared to seek a true marriage partner. She "needs" a man who will be a daddy to a little girl—a man who will listen to her, cuddle her, give to her, make her a queen the way Daddy always did. That's a bill no man her age can or should fill, so she's headed for eventual disappointment.

The irony is, these women aren't helpless babies. Their fathers have trained them well for many kinds of success in the world. The close relationship with Dad has given them excellent training in "competence," that is, a good handle on life skills like goal-setting, objectivity, leadership and initiative. As high schoolers they were often president of this club or that, and as adults they do well in the working world.

In a study of twenty-five high-level women executives, each woman attributed her success to what we'd call too-wonderful fathers. These dads loved them, praised them, trained them and encouraged them to resist the traditional constraints society puts on women. All twenty-five were firstborn girls. Other studies show that most fathers prefer a boy as their firstborn, so it is possible that some dads with a firstborn girl attempt to raise their daughter to be the boy they couldn't have. In the case of these women the training worked. Each of them attached very strongly in their early careers to a particular male boss. Once in the care of this father-substitute, they subordinated all other relationships to it. Not one of these women married until after the age of thirty-five. They simply felt there wasn't enough time or emotional energy to divide themselves between work and a relationship.

The key to the success of these women seems to rest in their relationship with their fathers, especially during adolescence. None of their mothers had particularly magnetic personalities. One described her mother as "a warm, fluffy pillow, not terribly exciting, while my father was always dynamic, a really charismatic personality."[1] When they were teenagers and their mothers attempted to channel them toward "ladylike behavior," these girls resisted, and got their fathers' support. Their fathers stepped in to teach them the skills and abilities they themselves used to make it in the world. Most of these women recalled talking over business interests with their fathers, and sharing recreational interests, too, like tennis and sailing. Each chose a co-educational university, preferring the company of men and a profession-oriented emphasis rather than liberal arts. For almost each one, her first work experience was in a position created for her as a favor to her father.

So it was Daddy who got them on their way professionally, and a daddy-substitute who took them to the top. For these women, the "love affair" with Daddy did not result in marital dissatisfaction, but that was mainly because they avoided marriage until later in life. But in their decisions, one might wonder if they really expressed a sense of personal identity, or if it was just their father's identity lived out through them.

What separates a too-wonderful father from an otherwise good father may be this: his closeness to his daughter

---

[1] Henning, Margaret and Jardin, Ann, *The Managerial Woman* (New York: Doubleday, 1981).

in contrast to his closeness to his wife. In response to the women executives' stories, one outsider observed, "One has the feeling these men were seeking in their daughters the comradeship they couldn't have with their more limited wives."[2] Henning's managerial women seemed to see their mothers as no rival for their father's attention. The contest had been won by the daughter years before.

Perhaps you enjoyed a close, special relationship with your father. But to determine if he was a too-wonderful dad, you might ask yourself, "If I had a daughter, and if my husband was as close to her as my dad was to me, how would I feel?" A father who prefers his daughter's company to that of his wife is asking for trouble.

The Daughter Who Is Needed Too Much

Another kind of too-wonderful father produces a daughter who is as frilly and feminine and as "all-girl" as the daughter we've just seen is businesslike and competent. This father needs too much to play the role of Rescuer, so instead of pushing his little girl out of the nest at the appropriate time, he keeps her dependent on him by overindulging her. He makes himself indispensable by lovingly undermining her attempts at acquiring professional competence or supportive peer relationships that will help her make it on her own. This daughter becomes the child-woman who can only survive if she has a man to care for her, and life without a man is unthinkable, or at least barely tolerable.

Elizabeth's doting father would only let his "little princess" leave the nest when he could give her to the care of a young man he'd "created." The boy was troubled and directionless when Elizabeth started bringing him home with her. Elizabeth's dad provided the fathering the boy

---

[2]Sheehy, Gail, *Passages* (New York: Bantam. 1977) p. 323.

had lacked in his own home, and the boy blossomed. Later, he and Elizabeth fell in love, and left for a job with an architectural design firm half a continent away. But their promising marriage fell apart before they'd seen two anniversaries pass, and Elizabeth came back home to Daddy, wringing out self-pitying tales of how much she'd done and how little her groom had done to make the marriage work.

She brought her stories to the right place. Daddy sympathized, bolstered her shattered ego, and sent her financially and emotionally refurbished back to school to pick up another degree. This further established her pattern of imbalanced male-dependency. At the university, Elizabeth met a divinity student. He was married, but when he graduated and took a pastorate several states away, Elizabeth packed up and followed him as church secretary. Incredibly, the young minister kept their relationship genuinely platonic. He appreciated her help without taking advantage of her need for him. They worked together until he was assigned a larger church in the denomination. Then Elizabeth simply transferred the loyalty she'd felt for him to another. When this attachment had to dissolve, several others like it followed. She'd join a church fellowship or a Christian singles' group long enough to attach to the male leader and seek out his attention under the guise of counseling for her numerous personal problems. When he (or his wife) grew tired of her dependence, Elizabeth would move on to another group.

She did marry again, this time to a charming musician—who couldn't find work. Elizabeth's dad is helping them financially "just until my husband's break comes," she says.

The Daughter Who Never Lets Her Father Fall From Grace

God intended that fathers *represent* God to their daughters—not that they *become* gods themselves. This is precisely the problem with a too-wonderful father. He enjoys his daughter's worship, and uses his power over her to position himself as an undefiled hero in her eyes. So when his adult daughter runs into difficulties, her gut reaction is, "If only Daddy were here!" Or when she marries, she expects her husband to be a Messiah to her, meeting all her needs, providing undivided attention and devotion, giving totally, with no needs of his own. If her man fails she feels she's married the wrong person. She may work at the marriage, but her forays to find counseling focus on how to change herself only insofar as that will make her husband change and meet more of her needs. It doesn't occur to her that she might seek help to learn to appropriate the grace and power of Christ in her own life. If you tell her it's possible in Christ to live satisfied and whole, even if her husband never changes, she has great difficulty believing you.

A full, beautiful, loving relationship between a father and his daughter is one of God's most wonderful treasures. But when we worship the gift instead of the Giver we destroy the beauty of the gift. It becomes an idol, a false god that will disappoint and fail us. In adolescence and beyond, a woman must see her father as he is, the vehicle for God's grace and help, God's instrument, not God himself. The wise and godly father knows he cannot be God to his daughter, and that she must learn to live with the dangers and challenges she must face without him if she's to become a godly adult.

The father who lets his daughter see his inadequacies, and allows her to get into situations where he can't rescue her is the father who launches her on toward her own life in God. She learns things he doesn't know, and he allows her to teach him. And he can look to God himself for help in filling the void he feels when she gives her love to the man she'll marry. He doesn't need to live for her, so he can set her free so that she does not have to live to please him.

A father who can let go sends his daughter out into life in the care of God. And if she needs a "launching" out of the nest, he provides the nudge. After she's gone, he makes sure her pleas for help don't always evoke an "I'll-be-right-over!" response from him. Instead, he consciously works at helping her solve her own problems, drawing on people and support besides his. He prepares her for inter-dependence, then grants her freedom gladly when she's ready.

What If He Was Never a Hero to Start With?

A girl can't gradually move away from her father if she never belonged to him in the beginning. The Distant Father, or the Unpleasable Father, or the Weak Father can't launch his daughter away from him and into adult life because they were never properly connected to start with. A woman can't successfully move away from what she never had.

She may leave home, but instead of a gradual emotional withdrawal from her father-dependency, her "launching" is more like being dumped out. Outwardly, she may speak of her father in vague terms, as if he's not a factor in her life at all, and never was. But inwardly, her life becomes a search to fill the inner hunger for the father-love she never experienced.

Breaking Up Is Hard to Do

Launching a child into the world at any age is difficult. It tore me to leave our two-year-old Scott with a Sunday-school teacher he didn't like. And I can still feel the wave of emotion that washed over me when our tiny five-year-old daughter climbed on that enormous yellow school bus bound for kindergarten. How much more wrenching it must be for a dad who has given nearly twenty years of training and caring to have to send his beloved daughter alone into a world he knows can be ruthless and devastating.

But it's also true that in order for that child to come more fully under the fatherhood of God, she must be rightly launched out into His care.

Yes, fathering gone awry can produce dismal effects in a daughter. But when a father supplies something of the four ingredients of effective fathering, he provides a setting in which his daughter can grow toward wholeness—and toward the Lord.

After all this talk about good fathering, are you wondering how your father rated? If so, the fathering inventory you'll find in the next chapter can help you evaluate your life together.

◇ 6 ◇

Who Was That Masked Man?

What are your memories of your father? How accurate are they? "The past" is sometimes a strange thing, as my friend Valerie discovered. Valerie is intrigued by the past, and her house shows it. Most of her furniture came straight from antique shops, and she has the only living room I've ever seen that's decorated with a life-sized mannequin in a sixty-year-old satin and lace wedding gown.

With such a passion for the past, Val couldn't say no when the manager of a nearby historical site called and asked her to spend a day giving tourists a taste of the life of a farmwife at the turn of the century. This invitation to the "good old days" stirred up Val's sense of nostalgic romance—took her back to the pre-polyester pleasures of swishing about in delicate, vintage clothing while sipping apple cider fresh from the press. She couldn't resist bringing her husband in on the fun.

The day Val and her husband played farm couple, however, the tomato crop was "coming on," so she had to spend the entire day canning. Unfortunately, on this particular July morning the temperatures soared to 105 degrees. So after hours of leaning over a wood-burning cookstove in an *un*air-conditioned kitchen tending to steamy kettles of stewing tomatoes, Val was sure the thermometers had hit *155!* By noon, her long cotton skirt stuck to her sweaty legs, and the makeup she'd applied that morning was dripping from her face. And she got no sympathy from her husband, because he'd spent that blistering morning chopping wood, and felt the need of some sympathy himself!

They tried to escape the oppressive kitchen by taking their meal outside, but the flies were so thick they were driven back indoors. So they suffered through bowls of hot stew (no cold lunch without refrigeration), after which Val's husband escaped the kitchen before she fired up the stove again, heating water to wash the dishes.

That evening, two exhausted but more realistic people went back to their suburban comfort, giving thanks for air-conditioning, ice-cold sodas, and microwaves. Val learned the hard way that her mental picture of the good old days simply wasn't accurate. She knew part of the truth about the past, perhaps, but not the whole truth.

The same can be true for your memories of growing up. I found this as I personally interviewed many women about their fathers. We'd discuss the four ingredients of effective fathering—involvement, warmth, discipline, and launching. But when I'd ask for an assessment of how their father rated in these areas, women would often draw a blank. Or else they'd evaluate their father's behavior as "good" in an area, but then go on to describe scenes from childhood that contradicted their evaluation. Occasionally, I also saw the reverse to be true.

In truth, it seemed that these women had actually thought so little about their personal interactions with their fathers that it was difficult to evaluate them accurately. Or, for reasons we'll touch more on later, they'd either idealized their father, or made him worse than he actually was.

Trying to rate how warm your father was toward you isn't easy. It's much easier to recall accurately whether he usually spoke to you in a friendly voice, for example. On the following pages, you will find an inventory that's designed to help you get a clearer image of your dad, one that's less distorted, perhaps, by layers of distance and emotion.[1]

To get the best picture, you will want to answer these questions in light of your father's behavior toward you when you were young. One woman told me, "When I'm with Daddy, he always cries when I get ready to leave. Of course he's in his seventies, and it's very real to him that with his children as geographically scattered as we are, there is the chance he could die before he would see us again."

I don't know if her father also cried when she was ten and left the house, but her response illustrates an important point. During the years we've been growing up, our fathers have been changing as well. Most likely, they're not the same at seventy as they were at thirty. But how *we* were shaped depends more on how they behaved at thirty, so it's vital to remind yourself to look back.

While you're doing the inventory, it may help to take a moment, close your eyes and let your mind go back to when you were eight or ten. Envision your home, and see your family in a favorite room in that home. If your father was living with your family, picture him in your mind. If your father died or left before this time in your life, base your answers on what you can remember of him.

---

[1]The format for this inventory was inspired by a psychological test called "Parent Behavior Inventory," developed by Earl S. Schaefer at the National Institute of Health. Dr. Schaefer's parenting model differed significantly from mine, so the concepts for which he was testing couldn't be applied directly to what I was trying to do. But his methods in creating the inventory served as a guide, and some of the ideas for specific items were adapted from his inventory.

I'm also indebted to Dr. Robert Hutzell, clinical psychologist and director of a behavioral health clinic, for his advice in designing and testing this tool.

Fathering Inventory

Each of the four ingredients of effective fathering has ten items listed under it. Each item describes a way your father may have behaved toward you *when you were a child.* If you think the item was LIKE your father, you simply circle *L.* If you think it sounds only SOMEWHAT LIKE your father, circle *SL.* If it is NOT LIKE your experience with your father, circle *NL.* Now go ahead and rate your father on the following behaviors.

SCORING:

Add up the numbers under the answers you circled for each of the four sections of the inventory, and record them below.

INVOLVEMENT _____

WARMTH _____

DISCIPLINE _____

LAUNCHING _____

Involvement

		L	SL	NL
1.	Seemed to think of me often	10	5	0
2.	Didn't talk with me very much	0	5	10
3.	Seemed to enjoy doing things with me	10	5	0
4.	Complained that I got on his nerves	0	5	10
5.	Was interested in meeting my friends	10	5	0
6.	Hardly noticed when I did well at home or at school	0	5	10
7.	Talked things over with me	10	5	0
8.	Didn't help me when I needed it	0	5	10
9.	Enjoyed going on drives, picnics, or trips with me	10	5	0
10.	Spent very little time with me	0	5	10

Warmth

1. Made me feel better after talking over my worries with him	L 10	SL 5	NL 0
2. Seemed to see my faults more than my good points	L 0	SL 5	NL 10
3. Almost always spoke to me with a warm, friendly voice	L 10	SL 5	NL 0
4. Thought my ideas were silly	L 0	SL 5	NL 10
5. Hugged and kissed me often	L 10	SL 5	NL 0
6. Wished I was different from what I was like	L 0	SL 5	NL 10
7. Told me I was good-looking	L 10	SL 5	NL 0
8. Rarely praised me	L 0	SL 5	NL 10
9. Seemed happy to see me	L 10	SL 5	NL 0
10. Didn't understand what mattered to me	L 0	SL 5	NL 10

Discipline

	L	SL	NL
1. Insisted I obey, even if I complained or protested	10	5	0
2. Let me off easy when I did something wrong	0	5	10
3. Saw to it that I knew what was expected of me	10	5	0
4. Gave me as much freedom as I wanted	0	5	10
5. Insisted I complete work I'd been assigned	10	5	0
6. Didn't pay much attention to my misbehavior	0	5	10
7. Chose reasonable punishments for me	10	5	0
8. Made excuses for my bad behavior	0	5	10
9. Saw to it that I obeyed when he told me to do something	10	5	0
10. Could be talked into things easily	0	5	10

Launching

1. Always told me why his way was best	L 0	SL 5	NL 10
2. Had to know exactly where I went and what I had been doing and with whom	L 0	SL 5	NL 10
3. Let me have a say in how to do things we worked on	L 10	SL 5	NL 0
4. Usually made me the center of his attention at home	L 0	SL 5	NL 10
5. Let me do normal things most other children my age did	L 10	SL 5	NL 0
6. Wished I could stay at home where he could take care of me	L 0	SL 5	NL 10
7. Felt sure I could take care of myself even if he wasn't around to help	L 10	SL 5	NL 0
8. Made me feel I was the most important person in his life	L 0	SL 5	NL 10
9. Cared whether I knew skills for independence, like balancing a checkbook, etc.	L 10	SL 5	NL 0
10. Seemed crushed if I didn't always follow his advice	L 0	SL 5	NL 10

Evaluating Your Responses

On each section of the inventory, the highest score possible was 100, the lowest 0.

What is most significant about your score from this father inventory is how they stand in relation to *each other*. If your father scored a 5 on nearly every item—but, in one category went up to all 10s, or down to near 0, this area was likely the most influential one to you growing up. A pastor's wife gave her father scores in the 40s and 50s for every area of fathering except discipline, where his score zoomed to a perfect 100. It's not hard to imagine his firmness would have played a major part in shaping his daughter's adult life.

If you didn't see any clear pattern in your scores, or if the scores and your memories seem at odds, two factors may be significant.

First, remember that there's no room in the test to explore your father's motives for his behavior. Traci's father rated relatively high on warmth, but she explained to me later that his "warmth" was actually an attempt at emotional and sexual exploitation. The notes she penciled onto her inventory told the true story, like this:

"Almost always spoke to me with a warm, friendly voice" (Bordering on seduction)

"Hugged and kissed me often" (He would have loved more!)

"Told me I was good-looking" (Constantly leered at me)

"Seemed happy to see me" (Wanted *me* to feel the same)

As with Traci, it's possible that your father's fathering was laced with hidden agendas and double messages.

There is a second reason why scores may not mesh with the reality you recall.

One woman who took this inventory ended up with all her scores above 75. On warmth, her father rated a glowing 90. Yet in her adult life she had severe problems relating to men, and her marriage had been going through ups and downs for a number of years. This woman had chosen to idealize the past because she feared the pain that might come if she looked reality in the face. Some of us have reasons like this, or others, for not seeing our father for who he really was to us.

Putting the twenty or thirty more years you spent with your father into an objective light may be one of the most difficult things you've done to date. What makes it so confusing?

Five Reasons Why It's Hard to See Dad Objectively

First, your father may have treated you differently at different periods in your life. How you were treated in a developmental period can have profound effects.

Medically—by way of example—obstetricians across the country have issued stern warnings to their pregnant patients about the dangers of drinking alcohol. Even a small amount of alcohol can affect a growing fetus in catastrophic ways. Why? Because those early weeks of life, particularly during the first trimester, constitute a critical period of development for the organ systems of the body. Enormous changes are taking place very quickly, and the effects of those changes will shape the child's bodily functioning for the rest of her life.

Psychologists believe we have critical periods like this in our emotional development as well. There are certain times—not necessarily the same times for everyone—when *future* emotional security hinges on how effectively our needs were met *right then.*

For a girl's relationship with her father, one of those critical periods seems to appear when she is three to five years old. The other is at adolescence. Though interactions with her father will influence development all along, there appears to be a special sensitivity toward the input her dad has to offer during these two critical periods. During these times, the growing girl has a special awareness of gender differences, and is particularly susceptible to being molded in her expectations and images of herself as female.

Audrey's dad loved babies, so after Audrey was born, Tim ran circles around the other neighborhood daddies, plying her with gifts, bragging about her accomplishments, shuttling her to the zoo and ball games and swimming lessons. As "Daddy's Girl," Audrey blossomed in the warmth of his attention.

But about the time Audrey started wearing a bra, she lost her daddy. He was still there physically, but the warmth and teasing and hugging between them screeched to a halt. A little girl was one thing, but now Timothy's daughter was suddenly becoming a woman, and her emerging sexuality frightened him. In reaction, he withdrew, leaving Audrey confused and insecure.

Girls like Audrey abound.[2] Dr. Trobisch found that 40 percent of the women he studied experienced just such a change in the relationship with their fathers. If your father related differently to you at different points in your life, you may have trouble clearly defining who he was to you.

---

[2]Dr. Margo Maine, a specialist in eating disorders at Children's Hospital in Newington, Conn., sees girls like this continually in her work with anorectics.

In a study of thirty-nine girls with anorexia, nearly all had fathers who gave them little emotional support. And almost half of the fathers demonstrated the pattern Audrey's father did of withdrawing from their daughters when the girls reached puberty. These girls, aware of their fathers' withdrawal, reasoned that sexual development must mean losing Dad. And on some level, they decided that if they regressed back to childhood, they could win him back. Starving themselves seemed to be an attempt to regain the little girl body they were losing, and thus to hold on to their father's love. (Reported by Mary Mohler, "A New Look at Anorexia," *Ladies Home Journal,* April 1986, 74.)

Second, he may have related to you differently than he did to your other brothers or sisters.

When Barbara's father came in the front door at 5:30 each evening, his interactions with his three children followed a well-established pattern. He'd shuffle past eldest daughter Melissa with barely a grunt of recognition. Younger daughter Barbara would receive a slight smile or a sentence response—depending on how hard she decided to work that day at being "Daddy's Sunshine Girl." But for Bart, the long-awaited and treasured son, their father *always* had an affectionate greeting.

If these three siblings described their relationship to their father, we'd get three different stories. And sometimes a father might behave the same toward each of his children, but each child responds differently.

Counselor Earnie Larsen observes:

> Brothers and sisters growing up in the same family come out with vastly different messages and patterns [from their parents]. Of two children who grew up in a very assertive or aggressive kind of family, one may well grow up taking on that pattern and become a very self-centered, aggressive and controlling person. The other child may come out very fearful, very passive, very intimidated and very willing to lie down and be a doormat. Your brothers and sisters may not have learned at all the same things you learned. Response can be affected by birth order, sex, size and intelligence.[3]

Trusting your own perceptions of your relationship with your father rather than relying on your brother's or sister's interpretation will help in getting a clearer picture of the influence your father had on you.

---

[3]Earnie Larsen, *Why Does This Always Happen to Me?* Booklet 2 of the series, "I Should Be Happy ... Why Do I Hurt?" (St. Paul, Minn.: International Marriage Encounter, copyright, 1986), 6.

Third, your father may have had a "split personality," so to speak.

As one woman said, "A high school friend of mine once told me, 'Your father is so much fun!' I thought, *Is she talking about my dad?* Around home he was always in a bad mood and critical of everything. But I guess he didn't show that part of himself to outsiders."

Also, some dads have exemplary characters, but simply aren't terrific fathers. I believe the Old Testament prophet Samuel was one such man. Samuel stood courageously for God's truth, yet his children didn't follow the Lord (1 Samuel 8:3). David was another who modeled godliness in his work, but who largely failed as a father.

If your father behaved differently with others than he did with your family, or didn't do well at fathering even though you respect him for other qualities, it may take time to sort out the different pictures you carry of him, so you can look realistically at your relationship to him and how it affected your life.

Fourth, you may be from a home where the truth was not told.

Many families operate under the illusion that if negative behavior isn't called what it is, the children won't be affected by it.

One daughter of an alcoholic father said, "No matter what he did or said, no matter how 'crazy' he acted, we pretended nothing happened. We never discussed the reason for his behavior. I went through a brief period of drinking too much myself. My mother was very upset about it. But even then she didn't tell me why, she didn't say up front, 'The reason I'm so upset is that your father is an alcoholic and I'm afraid it could happen to you.' "[4]

---

[4]Margaret Jaworski, "Growing Up With Alcoholism," *Family Circle* (April 15, 1986), 20.

Fifth, you may be forgetting memories too painful to remember.

In a fight scene from one of Sylvester Stallone's infamous *Rocky* movies, the bell signals the end of a round in the boxing match, and Rocky staggers to his corner and collapses. As his eyes swell shut and his mouth bleeds, his manager yells in the boxer's face, *"No pain! No pain!"*

"No pain," Rocky mumbles as he staggers to his feet to take another battery of brutal blows.

Denial can hide pain, but it also makes accurate memories of the past more difficult to recall. And it won't do much to lead us into wholeness.

Some women who were sexually abused as children can go for years with no conscious recollection of the abuse. One woman reported not being able to remember entire summers of her childhood, and barely any of her high school years at all. But her amnesia made sense when it finally became known that during those years she'd been repeatedly molested by her father. Perhaps it is a woman like this who author Nancy Friday describes when she writes, "She will see in those early years only what she can afford to live with."[5]

Other women bury *positive* memories of their fathers. Why?

For one thing, carrying grudges will tend to color our memories, turning a weakness-prone but well-intentioned father into a malicious ogre. Or wrongly accusing Dad of neglect may be a ploy to keep us from having to face our own problems. Painting an unrealistically dark picture of the past can get us sympathy and attention ("You poor, abused child . . ."). And pity feels good to some women, even though it thwarts growth. We might be giving in to ungratefulness or bitterness, which can cause us to over-

---

[5]Nancy Friday, *My Mother, Myself* (New York: Delacorte Press, 1977), 49.

look any good our fathers might have offered us.

Or maybe we look at the past too negatively because we simply expected too much. We wanted a human father who was God-perfect. Many of us have grown up in the generation that has decided to "have it all." We believe we deserved only the best because we are "worth it"—or so the hair coloring commercials tell us. Perhaps we think we deserved perfect parenting, as well.

Whether we deny reality by making the past too glowing or too sour, denial can be a potent factor that can keep you from seeing your relationship to your father as it really was.

There are other issues involved in looking back. In the next chapter, we will explore your mother's role, and then investigate ways to use the information you cull from your past to stimulate your present growth.

Looking back may be some of the most growth-producing work you can do. At least my friend Judy would say it is. Several years ago, Judy sat in a family therapist's office trying to clarify the anger she felt toward her husband. In the course of their conversation, her therapist prodded Judy to look back at the family in which she grew up. And as they explored her destructive relationship to an abusive father, the therapist finally observed, "It looks to me as if you're mad at the wrong man!"

He turned out to be very right. Making her way through the mountain of shame, and anger and confusion she felt toward her father has taken Judy years of work, but she's moving toward freedom. And peace. And wholeness.

Perhaps, like Judy, you need to take a long, honest look back in preparation for the journey forward.

◊ **7** ◊

Your Father and His Wife

For a number of years, the popular Christian family advisor Charlie Shedd served on the board of a psychiatric hospital. While there, he heard a lecture that changed his approach to parenting. The subject was "The Importance of Parental Harmony as the Primary Source of Emotional Stability in the Growing Child." From that lecture, Shedd concluded that his number-one job as a father was not to provide food and shelter. Not to protect his children. Not to be a good example, or to administer discipline. His primary job, he decided, was to love his children's mother well.

"I regret to report that up until then I had never given it a thought," Charlie Shedd said later. "And when I began to ponder this insight, I discovered an awful truth—I was a lousy lover! It wasn't that I didn't love their mother. It was simply that I had let that fact be crowded out by other facts. I went to Martha with the biggest 'I'm sorry' ever."

Shedd followed his apology with a two-step plan for change. First, the Shedds committed themselves to going out together for dinner alone once a week. No guests. No

72

entertaining. Second, they planned on fifteen minutes a day of visiting in-depth. "This is not small talk about bills, the kids, planning the weekend," he explained. "The subject now is what's going on inside."[1]

In learning to love his wife first and best, Charlie Shedd was also giving a priceless gift to his daughter. A dad who honors his wife, respects women, and cares for his daughter broadcasts a congruent message of worth that trumpets too loudly to be missed.

When a Swedish researcher interviewed pregnant girls and their mothers, he found that unhappy homes produce daughters with disrupted relationships with men. Compared to girls from peaceful homes, the girls raised in what he called "discordant" upbringing had less stable and satisfying relationships with men, and had more sex partners by the time of their first pregnancy. They were also less likely to consistently achieve orgasm.

But most importantly, when the girls' parents fought, daughters more frequently reported feeling estranged from their *fathers,* and much less frequently from their mothers.

We've learned to see womanhood through the lens of our father's relationship to his wife, and her attitude toward him, as well.

What Was Your Father's "Message" to You?

Pretend for a moment that everything you know about the value of women was suddenly erased from your mind. Then imagine that the only way you can judge what you were worth as a female was to observe how your father treated other women, especially your mother.

What conclusions would you come to? If your father had been Charlie Shedd, you might expect being a woman

---
[1]Charlie Shedd, *The Best Dad Is a Good Lover* (New York: Avon Books, 1978), 9–10.

to be a positive experience. You'd be prepared to receive kindness, respect, and a sense of true partnership from the men you encountered. And from your husband, you'd expect to be esteemed and loved.

Are these the things you learned as you observed your father and mother living together?

Your relationship with your father didn't exist in a vacuum. How he interacted with your mother—and with other women, too—may have had an enormous influence on the woman you are today.

Message From an Unfaithful Husband

Wendy said, "I never remember my father having a kind word for my mother. According to him, meals were always planned wrong, cooked wrong, served wrong. When she cleaned the house, he let her know she didn't do it often enough. When she dressed up, he criticized her choice of clothes, or her makeup. He laughed at her ideas and cut down her initiatives. I often wonder if this has anything to do with why I struggle so much with feeling that motherhood can't be a worthwhile way to spend my time!"

Adding to her confusion, the only women Wendy's dad praised were overtly sexy ones. He loved smirking at off-color jokes about women who represented the opposite of everything Wendy's mother did. Though no hard evidence ever emerged of affairs, it was clear to the family and their friends that Wendy's mother wasn't attractive to her husband, and other women most definitely were.

The message that came through to Wendy was this: Without physical attractiveness and freedom from children, there would be no chance of getting and keeping a man's love.

"For years I resisted the idea of having children,"

Wendy says. "I believed God wanted my husband and me to begin a family, yet when I became pregnant I went into a deep depression. It took months of searching to understand my feelings. I was afraid that if we had children, eventually my husband would lose interest in me—just the way my father lost interest in my mother. Oh, I covered my resistance to childbearing under a mountain of self-fulfillment rhetoric, and talked about 'not ever having a motherhood dream.' But underneath I feared repeating my mother's life, and being treated as shabbily as she was. If my father had only respected her, what a difference it would have made for me!"

Message From a Domineering Husband

Maureen Green, in her book *Goodbye, Father,* observes: "The kind of husband who contradicts everything his wife says, changes her decisions, and takes every opportunity to degrade and humiliate her in front of the children is bringing up his daughter for the psychiatric ward."[2] Green may be overstating her case, but the problem she's highlighting isn't exaggerated.

Some of the unhappiest women I have interviewed had similar answers when I asked, "What is your dad's attitude toward females?" They'd say, "He thinks women are dumb and worthless—unless of course they're serving men." Or, "Women aren't as good as men, but that didn't include me, *as long as I did what he said.*" These women didn't expect to be heard in the world of men unless they could "out-man" the men they worked and lived with.

The message this father sends is: Women are not supposed to think.

[2]Maureen Green, *Goodbye, Father* (London and Henley: Routledge and Kegan Paul, 1976), 14.

Message From an Uninvolved Husband

Marla's mother ran the family, pushing both her husband and children to live up to her expectations. She decided how the money would be spent, how the house would be decorated, how they'd vacation, who they'd socialize with. Marla's father retreated into workaholism.

Marla says, "I saw early on that Dad wasn't going to do anything to stop Mom from bulldozing over all of us. Sure, he was nice enough, but I concluded from what he didn't do that men can't be counted on when the going gets tough."

Candy, whose father was a workaholic, recalls her mother berating herself for her lack of value. "Daddy is the only important one," she'd say, "because he's making all the money. I don't really matter." And even when she became severely depressed and sought help from Candy's father, he merely ignored her.

The message from this type of father is this: A woman can't expect support from men if she struggles with domestic and emotional issues.

One woman with an uninvolved father put it this way. "I learned that women are the only dependable ones. Men are accidents looking for a place to happen."

Message From a Husband Who Puts His Daughter First

The fathers we've considered so far showed little respect for either their wives or daughters. But an equally damaging situation can develop when a father responded to his daughter *more* than he responded to his wife.

Such was Amanda's experience.

Amanda could have been a clone of her dad. The same electric blue eyes framed with a fringe of golden-blond hair. The same outgoing personality. The same "let's-jump-in-and-try-it" approach to life. From day one, her father adored her. Even when Amanda was still a tyke, he found her easier to be with than he did his wife, who always seemed to be so reluctant about everything. And so negative. Communication between them had become such hard work that he'd quit trying.

But Amanda was easier to talk with, and a whole lot more fun. Friends noticed how quick he was to praise his daughter, and promote her, and hug her. But they rarely heard praises for his wife, and never saw public demonstrations of affection for her.

The father we're describing wasn't a perpetrator of sexual abuse, or having a physically incestuous relationship. But one woman with this kind of father says, "What happened between us was actually emotional incest. My father pulled from me the warmth and communication and intellectual stimulation he wasn't getting in his relationship with my mother."

This woman's experience is not isolated. After reading Dr. Margaret Hennig's study of managerial women, all of whom had been strongly influenced by their fathers, one observer wrote: "One has the feeling these men were seeking in their daughters the comradeship they couldn't have with their more limited wives."[3]

Something has to be missing in a thirty- or forty-year-old man who prefers the companionship of an eight-year-old girl to that of a grown woman. Does he choose his daughter because he has to give so little to meet her expectations? Or is he threatened by the give-and-take of a mature, intimate relationship? Whatever the reason, his attention can leave his daughter feeling an uneasy mix of triumph and guilt.

---

[3]Gail Sheehy, *Passages* (New York: E.P. Dutton and Company, Inc., 1974), 323.

In her book *Like Father, Like Daughter,* Suzanne Fields explains: "[A father] provides a daughter with a sense of adventure and knowledge of sexual difference. If he spends a lot of time with her he will humanize the opposite sex for her, rather than causing her to idealize it. A father helps a daughter strengthen her sense of being female by providing a male self to see in contrast, but she must see this male affection in relation to her mother as well as having it directly expressed to her. . . . A father who spends time with his daughter instead of with his wife is courting trouble."[4]

When a dad is closer to his daughter than to his wife, he creates plenty of room for a girl to develop fears about her sexual development. She's won her dad intellectually and emotionally. Now that she's becoming a woman, might he prefer her sexually as well?

God intended that a father provide a safe testing ground for a young girl's emerging sexuality. Dr. John Musser explains that in a girl's innocent flirtations with her father, she gets to try out newly discovered skills without having to fear the repercussions. She knows he's committed to Mom, so she can "practice" womanly allure, all the while knowing there'll be no negative consequences. He's mature enough to affirm her femininity without making too much of her little advances. And his daughter knows she can't compete with Mom for his affection. Mom won his heart years ago, and still has it firmly for her own. At least that's how it should be. If it wasn't for her, you may have been left with great fears of your sexuality.

The message your dad gave you about your value has to be congruent with what you saw in his relationship to your mother, and to other women, before it can ring true

---

[4]Suzanne Fields, *Like Father, Like Daughter* (Boston: Little, Brown and Co., 1983), 74–77.

to you. But your mother played an active role, too, in shaping how you related to your dad. You received messages from her actions as well.

How Did Your Mother Relate to Your Father?

In his book *Father Power,* Dr. Henry Biller alerts men: "Your wife usually has a greater role in defining you to your children than you have in defining her. . . . One basis for your wife's high valuation of you as a father can be her high esteem for you as a husband. The happier the marriage, the better the father's relationship with his children is likely to be."[5]

Dr. Biller calls mothers "father-definers." For most of us, Mom was around more than Dad was, so much of our attitude toward him came filtered through what she thought of him.

For example, let's say he worked ten-hour days. She might have said, "We're so lucky to have a daddy who works this hard to provide for us." Or she could have said, "He's gone so much because he'd rather be with his cronies at work than here with us."

The way she chose to portray your father may have been accurate. Or it may have been better or worse than the truth. If she let you see him through rose-colored glasses, you may have a hard time now sorting the true from the false. And if she chose to make him out as a monster, or a lazy loafer, or as self-centered, she most likely helped to condition you to expect negative behavior from him, and perhaps from all men.

---

[5]Henry Biller, Ph.D., and Dennis Meredith, *Father Power* (New York: David McKay Co., Inc., 1974), 74.

Message From an Unhappy Wife

A couple's marital unhappiness particularly disrupts the children's relationship with their father. And daughters may be wounded by their parents' fighting even more than sons.

A group of researchers asked children ages seven to fifteen to describe how they felt about each of their parents. Then the researchers had two doctors and a nurse who knew the families judge the quality of the parents' relationships. When the marriage was rated a good one, girls talked about positive feelings toward their fathers. But when their parents' marriage was poor, girls—but not boys—reported negative feelings toward their fathers.

Author Maureen Green observes: "It is much easier for a malicious or simply unhappy mother to obstruct her daughter's feelings for her father; if she conveys to the young girl that men are frightening or despicable or simply inferior, and the father does nothing to break through to his daughter's understanding and win her sympathy, a girl may grow up permanently unable to understand or to tolerate the masculine point of view."[6]

Sometimes a negative portrayal of Dad is accurate. If it isn't, it can be a ploy, foisted on a daughter by a mother whose only sense of identity and worth rests in controlling her child. She sees a growing affection for Dad as a threat to her control over her daughter's love, and it frightens her.

The ultimate message reads something like this: Involvement with men leads to misery.

Message From a Supermom/Wife

One honest mother admits to feelings of jealously when her five-year-old daughter expresses her preference

---

[6]Maureen Green, *Goodbye, Father*, 76.

for her dad. "I set out to 'win' back her affections by out-daddying Dad. I insist on reading her the bedtime story every night. I strain my back carrying her on my shoulders. I walk her to school every day. Because I also hold a demanding job, I'm exhausted. But 'shared' parenting has turned sour. I don't want to share at the expense of my daughter's affections. I want total love from her, even if I have to be 'total mom' to get it."[7]

This mother realized in time her tendency to over-control. Less-perceptive or less-balanced mothers may go ahead and launch a subtle, yet full-scale campaign for control. They're willing to share the *chores* of child care with their husbands, but not the power to make decisions or claim affection from their daughters.

Women like this are probably much less numerous than fathers who simply don't want to take the effort to be involved. Yet these "Sabotage Moms" do create distance between a father and daughter that doesn't need to exist. As their daughters become women, they find they must circumvent (and sometimes anger) their mothers in order to get free and see their father as he is.

The reason she feels forced to choose is that Mom has spent a lot of effort to send this message: Loyalty to Dad equals disloyalty to me.

Message From a "Buffer" Wife

What happens when Mom insists on "translating" Dad to her daughter? Or when she seems afraid to let daughter and Dad confront each other?

Girls who grow up with a buffering Mom miss the chance to learn to work things out with a man. They often fear men's anger too much, or never learn to express their

---

[7]Ellen Sweet, " 'Mommy, I Love Daddy More,' " *Redbook* (May 1985), 112.

ideas with confidence to men.

As Joy says, "I'm always too fearful to tell men what I think. Or when I do, I come on too strong, because I expect they won't listen if I'm just myself. Because my mom 'protected' us from going directly to my dad about decisions or problems, I feel men won't be interested in my concerns. A little gruffness from men scares me off."

In their study of women without fathers, Elyce Wakerman and Holly Barrett observed that the world of childhood is largely a female domain. First at home, and then at school and church, it's women who direct and care for us. "Father," they write, "is a gift, a remote authority whose evening arrivals deliver us from the maternal bond, his encouragement suggesting our own possibilities in that other world: the world away from home and mother."[8] The authors then struggled to capsulize what it is that fatherless girls miss most. It was, they concluded, the "courage to dare." And some of this same courage may be dormant in girls who where always sheltered from interactions with their fathers by a buffering Mom.

Choosing the Messages You Receive

What did your father teach you about women, and therefore about yourself, by the way he related to your mother?

And what did you learn from your mother's attitude about your father and how he felt about you?

The father-daughter relationship is not a duet: It's a trio, at least. When you understand the messages you received from your parents about each other, only then can you begin to sort through them to settle on what was true, so you can live out your future freed by that truth.

---

[8]Elyce Wakerman, *Fatherloss* (Garden City, N.Y.: Doubleday and Co., 1984), 183.

◇ 8 ◇

Looking Back

Lila had just spent a week back at home in South Dakota, visiting her family. Some of the happenings of that visit dredged up reenactments of childhood put-downs from her sister and favoritism on her parents' part. Now she sighs, "I wonder if I ought to be doing all this digging around in the past. Sometimes I think it creates more problems than it solves."

Personally, as I have worked through my own past in relation to my family and my father, I have battled mentally with the same reluctance Lila feels. As a Christian, I've wondered: Are we bowing to Sigmund Freud, instead of to the Savior, when we look to the past? And is admitting our dads have in some ways behaved wrongly toward us a Christian response, or is it dishonoring?

Other Christians may struggle with these two questions, too. If you've asked these things, I offer some principles from Scripture for your consideration.

Christians are not supposed to deal with the past by ignoring it.

Paul wisely said, "One thing I do: Forgetting what is behind and straining toward what is ahead, I press on toward the goal" (Philippians 3:13, 14).

Some would say he's instructing us to stay away from the past so we can be free from it. However,

> you cannot forgive or forget what you have never re-called;
> you cannot leave a place you have never been;
> you cannot release what you have never held;
> you cannot seek healing for a wound you have not ac-knowledged.

Paul lived with an eye to the future, but he didn't *deny* or *ignore* his past, even the unsavory parts of his history. He acknowledged and accepted both his heritage as a Roman and a Pharisee, and even his years persecuting Christ's church. As he did, God used even the painful parts of Paul's background for His own purposes in advancing the Gospel.

God never intended we pretend offenses never happened. It's not un-Christian to say your dad was wrong.

Christian leader and author Elisabeth Elliot says this:

"There can be no forgiveness unless there is the acknowledgment that we have been sinned against. Forgiveness is not excusing. To excuse is to make nothing of the sin—to say, for example, he didn't mean to, or he couldn't help it, or he didn't mean it that way. Often this amounts to calling him irresponsible or immature. To forgive is first of all to face the truth: This thing was done to me; this man is responsible; it was wrong. Then it is to treat the person as though the things were never done and to be willing to be reconciled."[1]

The writer of Genesis shows this principle at work in the life of Joseph. Young Joseph was so hated by his jealous

---

[1]Elisabeth Elliot, *The Mark of a Man* (Old Tappan, N.J.: Fleming Revell Co., 1981), 139.

brothers that they sold him into slavery in a strange land. And if he had died there, his brothers would only have cheered.

But how could he rid himself of the anger? Was it by overlooking what they had done? By denying the pain they had caused him? By convincing himself they couldn't help it, or reminding himself they probably battled insecurity since Dad had loved him best?

None of the above! Joseph looked the pain they had caused him straight in the face, and gave them responsibility for the evil it really was.

"You intended to harm me," he said as they cowered before him, "but God intended it for good" (Genesis 50:20).

He did not say, "Don't feel bad. If you hadn't sold me into slavery, I'd never have wound up rich and powerful." Or, "Come on, guys. Boys will be boys. I'll bet if you'd known you were sending me off to misery and imprisonment, you'd never have done what you did. Right?"

No. Joseph looked at the past, and acknowledged the truth about their behavior toward him. "You intended to harm me . . ." From facing the truth, God could then take Joseph on to provide one of the most remarkable expressions of grace and mercy in the Bible.

The process of admitting the wounds your father intentionally or unintentionally inflicted may even cause you to feel angry for a time. This can be disturbing, because you may feel you're focusing only on the negative about your dad and his impact on you. But it is necessary to aggressively embrace the negative before you can in honesty and true forgiveness give credit for the positive.

A Look Back That Heals

Whether looking back leads to healing or not depends, I believe, on how it is done. Earnie Larsen, a Minnesota-based counselor with a particular interest in helping adult children of alcoholics, has developed some excellent guidelines for use as we look back at our fathering. They are as follows:

First, we're not looking for anyone to blame.

He explains: "The point of [looking back] is not to go back and blame and say, 'They did it to me.' As long as we are blaming someone else, we are passing off responsibilities. We don't go back to cast off responsibility, but rather to understand the patterns that still function and still dictate consequences in our lives, so that we can be more responsible, not less."[2]

Second, we don't go into the past to stay there.

My pastor in Kansas City told of a friend who traveled to the Holy Land and never came back. Yes, he re-boarded a plane and re-entered American air space, but mentally, he never made the trip home. After that vacation, it was nearly impossible to converse on any subject without his interjecting some reference to Israel. Friends saw his slide show until they weren't friendly anymore, and members of his congregation started placing bets on how early in the Sunday sermon his "when-I-was-in-the-Holy-Land" story would come.

It's possible to fall into the same trap as we look at our families. Larsen warns: "Some people get into [looking back], and for the rest of their lives they are shuffling through the past. Quite the opposite of going back there to stay, the reason we go back is precisely to be able to unhook from the past and to be able to get on with our lives. The reason is to discover, to understand, so we then

---

[2]Earnie Larsen, *Why Does This Always Happen to Me?* Booklet 2 of the series, "I Should Be Happy ... Why Do I Hurt?" (St. Paul, Minn.: International Marriage Encounter, copyright © 1986), 4, 5.

have the ability to let go of the past."[3]

Trust Christ for the help you need to see your father as he was to you. Some have found help in this journey from a close friend or counselor. But as you seek the right listening ear, be careful not to cast your pearls before swine. You'll need a listener who can accept both your positive and negative feelings without denying either.

We live in the Age of Therapy. Because there are more counseling options available than Baskin-Robbins has ice cream flavors, I'd like to digress for a moment and consider the factors involved in choosing a therapist if you decide to seek professional help.

Selecting a Therapist Means Asking Questions

Dr. Robert Hutzell, a clinical psychologist who has been in private practice, and now directs a group of psychologists in a clinic setting, would encourage you to ask questions.

Licensing standards for counselors vary immensely across the nation, so a listing in the Yellow Pages doesn't guarantee education or special training. (In Iowa, for example, anyone who wants to call himself a counselor can, so you could be seeing someone with years of training, or no special training at all.) Instead of simply getting a name from a friend or the phone book and setting up an appointment, Dr. Hutzell believes it wise to ask for a phone conversation with the therapist first.

During that visit, you'll want to ask about the therapist's education or credentials, and areas of expertise. You'll also want to describe your problem, to see if he or she feels comfortable dealing with it. (Some practices will provide a face-to-face consultation with the therapist at

---

[3]Ibid, 5.

no cost to exchange this same information.) You are, in a sense, interviewing the therapist, and giving him or her a chance to interview you, as well.

Dr. Hutzell also encourages patients to ask for a referral to another therapist if the counseling relationship doesn't seem to be connecting. "Asking for a change is usually more embarrassing to the patient than it is to the professional," he says. "Referring patients to another therapist isn't unusual, and a professional won't be threatened by your request."

If you are a Christian, you may feel more comfortable receiving help from someone who openly identifies himself as a Christian. Personally, when I felt I needed to talk about my spiritual struggles, I preferred a Christian counselor because I feared that with a counselor outside the faith, I'd be continually "editing" what I shared according to what impression it might be giving him of Christ: I wanted to be a "good witness."

But many people are helped immensely by secular counselors. It's possible to find a therapist who will treat your faith respectfully without embracing it. If you choose this route, remember this: Counseling does require a trust relationship in order to be most effective.

It's also important to connect with a counselor who places the responsibility for growth and change on you, rather than consciously or unconsciously seducing you into dependency on him or her.

It can be an incredible feeling to sit down with a sympathetic, attentive human being and to have them focus thoughts and energy on your concerns alone for fifty minutes, asking nothing in return but a check from your insurance company. It can, in fact, be addictive. A wise counselor will decide with you what problem you're there to solve, and how you'll both know when you're done.

I'm very grateful for the role counselors have played at

points in my journey. They've asked the questions I wouldn't have thought of asking, and suggested alternative solutions I couldn't have thought of trying. They've helped me get moving again when I felt bemired in a bog of negative feelings. You may well have the same experience.

Remember, too, that this decision about where to go for help is certainly worth praying about! The One who knows everything about you can guide you to the help you need in order to grow. He's interested in your past, because from it, He intends to shape your future.

Facing the Past Can Be a Tool to Grow Toward God

I've come to see that looking at your past isn't an elective in the school of spiritual growth: it's a requirement. Here are several reasons why this is so.

First, it is God's method of teaching us His ways.

"Listen to me, you who pursue righteousness and who seek the Lord: Look to the rock from which you were cut and to the quarry from which you were hewn; look to Abraham, your father, and to Sarah, who gave you birth. When I called him he was but one, and I blessed him and made him many. Surely the Lord will comfort Zion and will look with compassion on all her ruins" (Isaiah 51:1–3a).

So God commanded the children of Israel. He wanted memories of His faithfulness to their father to encourage them in a difficult time. God knows well the value of learning from the strengths of our fathers.

My father has always been a generous man. In retrospect, I've been amazed as I realize how difficult those choices to be generous must have been. My father worked two jobs most of his life to support the eight of us, and he could easily have used his limited income and family responsibilities as a reason not to give. But he didn't. My parents were firm on the issue of giving ten percent of their income to the church, and then to go beyond that to help whoever around them seemed to need it.

And somehow in the midst of it all, they managed to pay off the farm and help the six of us with college education. Through the way God blessed their generosity, I got to see firsthand that His promises to supply the needs of those who give really work! And their example has pushed me to give when I have feared we simply couldn't.

God intends we learn from our father's weakness, as well. In 1 Corinthians 10:1–11, Paul told the believers: "I do not want you to be ignorant of the fact, brothers, that our forefathers . . . drank from the spiritual rock. . . . Nevertheless, God was not pleased with most of them" (verses 1–5). Then Paul goes on to challenge his hearers to use their fathers' example as a warning, and to keep from setting their hearts on evil, as their fathers had done:

> Do not be idolaters, as some of them were. . . .
> We should not commit sexual immorality, as some of them did. . . .
> We should not test the Lord, as some of them did. . . .
> And do not grumble, as some of them did. . . .

Paul concludes, "These things happened to them as examples and were written down as warnings for us" (verse 11).

So even facing the family skeletons we'd rather keep locked away is also God's method of teaching us. Again in Hebrews, Paul tells about Israel's many rebellions in the wilderness, and then warns his hearers *not* to follow the example of their parents.

We want to identify what was right about our past,

but God also instructs us to face what was wrong. His purpose is not so we can find someone to blame for our irresponsible behavior, but rather to free us from unwittingly repeating wrongdoing.

Second, looking back can help us avoid repeating our fathers' mistakes.

Abraham's tenacious faith in God's promises served as a powerful example to his only son Isaac, and Isaac rightly followed his father's lead. But he imitated his father in another way, as well, and this time Abraham's example wasn't as praiseworthy.

Two different times, Abraham traded the promise of his wife's sexual favors to save his own neck. (See Genesis 12:10–20, and 20:1–17.) Only God's gracious intervention preserved Sarah's chastity.

And it seemed Isaac absorbed his father's weaknesses as well as he had his strengths. When he feared the Philistines might kill him to get his beautiful wife (exactly the fear Abraham had harbored about Sarah!), he lied and said she was his sister, thus making her fair game for the advances of the Philistine men. And in saying she was his sister, Isaac even fell back to the exact lie Abraham had used. (See Genesis 26:1–15.)

Is it any wonder that Jacob, Isaac's son, spent much of his life paying a heavy price for his own deceitful ways? His name even means "he deceives." His strong faith in God's promise followed family tradition, but this evil of lying passed from one generation to the next, as well. No wonder God tells us to remember the past, for negative lessons as well as positive.

We don't have to be enslaved to these family traditions. Just because your father saw fit to criticize those who didn't agree with him doesn't mean you have to do the same. But you won't begin to change until you stop calling his critical spirit "discernment," or his pride "self-confidence." Evils have to be identified before they can be forsaken.

Third, looking back prepares us to honor our fathers as God intends.

There must be something uniquely powerful in obeying the sixth commandment injunction to honor our fathers and mothers. It is the only commandment of the ten with a promise of blessing attached for obeying it. And it's the only commandment repeated again and again in the *New Testament.*

But when God instructs us to honor our fathers, He doesn't intend that we blindly worship them. God is not afraid of truth.

The Scripture says of David: "David . . . had not failed to keep any of the Lord's commands all the days of his life—except in the case of Uriah the Hittite" (1 Kings 15:5). Uriah, you may recall, was the man David had killed so he could steal Uriah's wife, Bathsheba. Even though God honored David above all others as a man after His own heart, He didn't gloss over David's wrong-doing. And because He didn't, we've learned as much from David's failure as we do from his successes.

In the same way, we don't dishonor our fathers by trying to see them objectively, as God sees them, any more than God dishonored David by exposing his sin with Bathsheba. Of course, if all we see of our fathers are their faults, then we've missed God's perspective also. David's sin was reprehensible, but God forgave him and spoke of him lovingly.

So it should be, ultimately, with our fathers.

Coming to terms with my father's shortcomings has freed me to honor him more than I ever did before. I know he isn't perfect, nor do I expect him to be anymore. He's just a human parent, like *me,* doing his best with the re-sources at hand—like *me.* With that view, I look with love and grace at how God used both what he was, and what he wasn't, to bring me to the heavenly Father.

As a result, seeing my dad as an instrument in God's hands lets me give him the place of honor God intended for him.

Blessed Are Those
Who Mourn

If your father—knowingly or unknowingly—was a source of emotional pain, you could be a woman with childhood voids that were never filled. Maybe you understand now that your father's failures have left you with insecurity, or feelings of worthlessness, or loneliness, or a shaky sense of confidence in your womanhood, or other wounds. But what now?

As one woman said, "I know the truth is supposed to make me free, but right now, it's mostly made me miserable!" She needs to know how to start moving in the direction of healing.

The first step in that journey toward healing probably isn't what you'd expect. The beginning of filling your fathering voids is to face them, feel them and let the depth of them surface. The process I'm describing is that of grief. It's what Anne Morrow Lindbergh pointed to when she said, "I do not believe that sheer suffering teaches. If suffering alone taught, all the world would be wise, since everyone suffers. To suffering must be added mourning. . . ."[1]

---
[1]Ingrid Trobisch, *Learning to Walk Alone* (Ann Arbor, Mich.: Servant Books, 1985), 65.

Alternatives to Mourning

Grieving our losses requires effort. But it's an effort we're not encouraged to expend because we live in an anesthetized society. We too quickly fill empty spaces with noise, activity, or "entertainment," and hope it will numb us to what hurts us. Maybe we try as hard as we do to cover up our pain because we don't know how to use the hurt constructively. We don't know why or how to mourn our disappointments, so we either let pain destroy us or we work very hard to ignore it.

There are many alternatives to constructively using the pain of disappointment. We can choose to settle into *anger and blaming*. Anger carries great power, so much that it seems to swallow up all the pain of loss. Many of the books I read about fathers and daughters stopped here, bemired in anger. "Because my father didn't love me . . . or encourage me . . . or stay with us . . . my life is ruined!"

Wailing ("if only") is another attempt at dulling pain. Those retreating into it wallow in the mire of senseless regrets and self-recrimination. "If only I'd had a more tender father, I could share my feelings more easily now. . . ."

Busyness is another alternative to facing our losses. Have you ever seen newly divorced men or women rush madly into a whirl of dating and going and doing in a frantic attempt to run away from pain? Those of us facing wounds from our growing-up years may try to pull off the same defense.

Inner deadness is a fourth way of escape. "My father wasn't the greatest, but it doesn't bother me." Psychologists call this isolation. We acknowledge our memories, but we take away their cutting edge by stripping them of any emotional content so they appear to have caused us no pain.

But at the death of Lazarus, the Bible tells us, "Jesus wept."

And when He received news of the horrible murder of His friend John the Baptist, Jesus left for a solitary place. I'm sure He went out alone to let the loss He felt at John's death pierce Him so He could receive God's comfort.

Much of the mourning for lost fathering isn't caused by the physical death of our dads, however. You may feel sadness for the loss of Dad's advice, or friendship, or help and protection, or wisdom, since each of these voids may have wounded you.

Some of our losses may seem deep, extreme, too much to bear. Such was the case of a woman referred to as "Marty." Ahead, you'll find her story in her own words. Though she faced memories of incest, and you may not have had her terrible experience, nonetheless, your pain may be just as real.[2] I believe Marty's ways of dealing with her grief are a good example of how to face wounds, but also how to open them to the Healer.[3]

One Woman's Mourning

When, after more than thirty years of amnesia and three years of therapy, I finally was able to remember the abuse of my childhood, part of me longed for some ritual to bring me closure to this part of my life, to celebrate the present, and to prepare the way to get on with the future.

I found myself wanting those social customs that someone receives who has had a child die, because a part of me, my child, was killed. In our area, it is the custom to have announcements printed up on little cards, telling of a person's death and funeral services. These cards are placed in local stores and mark the public

---

[2]For women who share Marty's experience of sexual abuse, I recommend the book *Child Sexual Abuses: A Hope for Healing* by Maxine Hancock and Karen Burton Mains (Harold Shaw Publishers, Wheaton, Ill., 1987).

[3]Marty Green, pseudonym, "Liturgy for a Lost Childhood," *Praying* (September 10, 1986), 19, 30.

acknowledgment that a loss has occurred. I wanted that public acknowledgment. I wanted neighbors to bring home-baked goods to the house, to have a wake and a funeral. I wanted my family to grieve with me. That isn't going to happen. Instead, a prayer emerged from inside of me.

The Prayer

God, my heart is surely broken. It is so hard to trust others, even you. Help me be open. Help me understand, too, about anger. I am so angry at *him* for what he did to me. I am so angry at *them* that I never even knew I deserved their love. And I was taught that anger is a sin. Admitting this rage makes me feel evil all over again. I need to learn it is part of being human, not a sign of my wickedness. Help, God.

Marty, listen to me. You have a right to your anger. Your loss is tremendous, but I do understand. I will help you heal.

But, God, I missed out on so much. I want to have a happy childhood. I want a mother and father who love me. Oh, God, I want what I can never have.

What they did to you is wrong. But now you are making your own choices for the future. You are building a new life in the light of my love. I am very proud of you. Do not despair. I have been with you and I promise to remain with you.

I want to believe. Each day I choose for the future, but it is so hard to remember the pain and anger that sometimes I can't let it go for fear of forgetting again. How do I live without pain, without anger, without a family? I just can't do it myself.

I promise you this; I am your light and your salvation. You need not fear. I will never leave you. I will never desert you. Even though your father and mother deserted you, I will always care for you. You can believe me; you will see goodness in life. Put your hope in me. Be strong.

I do try, God, but I feel such overwhelming failure. Again and again, I slip back and no longer want to live.

Please, God, are you sure it's worth the struggle? Do you even remember that I'm here?

Hush, Marty. Does a woman forget her baby, or fail to cherish the daughter of her womb? Yet even if these forget, I will never forget you. It will be all right. I'm here.

Okay, I will begin again, God. While the source of pain was forgotten, I could not heal. Now I know. Thank you, God, that I now know. Thanks for the memories. You always did know and you never left me. I don't understand that very much, but thank you. I will try to believe in you and—so much harder—try to believe in myself. Together we will heal, one day at a time.

God Wants Us to Be Honest

The words you've read show an honest grief in process. In opening her heart, Marty has taken a step few of us have the courage for, and I believe her honest expression brought great pleasure to God. When C.S. Lewis wrote down his feelings after the death of his beloved wife, Joy, he published those reactions under a pen name, because he feared they sounded too "un-Christian" for his readers to accept from one who professed faith in Christ.

However, in the book of Job, and in the Psalms, you'll find people of God railing, and moaning, and accusing, and doubting as they struggle through their disappointments and losses toward faith in God. And each of these who took their anger and guilt and doubts to God found Him ready to respond.

The wonderful truth is that God is ready to comfort us. Jesus said, "Blessed are those who mourn, for they will be comforted." It is only to those with the courage and faith to grieve their losses that Jesus promised comfort. And when we have looked the pain of damaged dreams full in the face, their power over us lessens. Perhaps that stands as a good definition of grieving: looking our loss full in the face.

When we do, God comforts us. One of my favorite pictures of God is drawn in 2 Corinthians 1:3, which speaks of Him as "the Father of mercies and God of all comfort, who comforts us in all our affliction." Maybe this particular name of God speaks to me because growing up, my sister and I shared an unheated bedroom in the upstairs of an old farmhouse. During the winter, the idea of being sent to our room as punishment would have been punishment, indeed, because it was frosty up there! From November to March we rarely entered the room except to hop into bed. And during those months, what protected us from the cold nights was a stack of fat patchwork comforters quilted by my grandmother. I can close my eyes still and remember sliding under those quilts and cuddling in like a caterpillar snuggling into a cocoon. God wants to be my comforter against the cold of sorrow and loss. He wants to protect and warm me, and give me rest. He is a solace and hiding place, and very near to those who mourn.

How to Mourn

Grief counselors say they observe three steps as a healthy grief moves toward resolution.

The first step is admitting the pain.

Ingrid Trobisch wrote: "My father had died and was buried in a lonely grave during World War II in Dar es Salaam, East Africa. I was only sixteen at the time of his death and had been deprived of his caring presence during those precious teenage years when a daughter desperately needs her father's love and affirmation. I can't remember weeping when we received the news of his sudden death.

I kept a stiff upper lip and thought my job was to comfort my mother and younger brothers and sisters. My father had always been my hero. I suppose that by not allowing myself to grieve for him, I was trying to be a hero too.

"One day, thirty years later, I was alone at the Lichtenberg. I remember watching the movie version of *A Tree Grows in Brooklyn* on television. All the floodgates in my heart broke loose as I empathized with the twelve-year-old girl weeping for her dead father. It seemed hours before I could stop crying. I realize now that this was a preparation for the loss of my husband a few years later. How, otherwise, could I have coped with a new loss if I had not grieved for the first loss?"[4]

Mrs. Trobisch understood the importance of letting herself admit the pain of loss, even a loss so deeply in the past.*

The second step in mourning is feeling the pain of loss.

After looking back at ways her father had affected her, a woman wrote to me, "My mourning has been not over actual past events, but over [the death of] illusions like . . .

"I'm an extremely mature and together person.
I wasn't affected by my past. I'm amazing.
My dad is just an innocent little boy who needs me.
My mother did the best she could.
I've forgiven and forgotten.
I don't need anyone."

She went on to describe her feelings this way: "I have gone on a life-changing journey, one that has dropped me over more cliffs than I would have ever jumped off voluntarily. I've confronted my mother, my memories, my

---

[4]Trobisch, 90.

*Women whose fathers have died will find a helpful resource in the book *Fatherloss: Daughters Discuss the Man That Got Away* by Elyce Wakerman (Garden City, N.Y.: Doubleday and Co., 1984).

shame, my fear, my sinful self-protective styles of relating to men and women, my longings, my rage, my vulnerability, my tears. And throughout I have run up against giant doubts and questions where God is concerned.

"[But] He gave me enough courage to get started on the journey." Then she admitted: "Nothing in my life has taken more courage than to live honestly through the past five months." And courage is what it takes to face pain.

I didn't think I felt any loss as I identified weaknesses in my relationship with my father. However, when I began interviewing women about their dads, I was surprised at my gut reactions to their stories. When I'd come across a woman who'd had idyllic fathering, I found myself picking at her. I liked these women least of any I spoke with. Later the light dawned. These women weren't categorically unlikable—I was just jealous of the closeness they had with their dads, and didn't want to admit it! My attitude told me I harbored wounds I was trying to ignore.

Letting your pain surface may mean saying, "I hurt," or "I'm angry," or "I'm disappointed." Many women find comfort in writing down their feelings. Others talk about them with a trusted listener.

The final step in mourning is letting go of all the pain.

And in the chapters ahead you'll discover ways to move beyond mourning as you find ways to forgive your father, and see how God wants to father you through His Word and His family.

But for now, remember this: There is strength enough in Jesus Christ to mourn the death of your illusion of having had a perfect father. God has promised, "When you pass through the rivers, they will not sweep over you. When you walk through the fire you will not be burned" (Isaiah 43:2). When you let the pain of your loss touch you, you can become free to let it go. Your disappointment need not be denied, or trivialized, or glossed over. It can be—it must be—mourned to begin to see it healed.

Considering a Confrontation

Understanding your pain inevitably leads to one question: Should you tell your father about it? H. Norman Wright, a marriage and family counselor, offers advice on this question in his excellent book *Always Daddy's Girl.*[5]

He asks several questions as women think about ways their dads have wounded them, such as:

What experiences would you like to discuss with your father?

What do you hope to accomplish by sharing them with him?

How do you hope he will respond?

How might you be different if you share these experiences with him?

How will you handle it if he does not respond positively when you share with him? Can you share your feelings with him for your own benefit and be satisfied regardless of his response?

These questions are vital, because not every daughter comes away jubilant from a confrontation with her father.

Janet's father left her mother when Janet was a year old, and as she grew up she became first her daddy's pretty little girl, then later his little woman. By the time she was thirteen he expected her to be his best listening ear, expert counselor and sex therapist. Their times together consisted solely of his pouring out his troubles with the dozens of women he had dated and slept with.

---

[5]H. Norman Wright, *Always Daddy's Girl* (Ventura, Calif.: Regal Books, 1989).

Janet said, "About a year ago, when events caused me to begin taking a serious look at my past, my sexuality and my deepest feelings, I told him—not in anger, but almost pleadingly—that I didn't want to hear any more about his sexual problems or opinions. After ripping me to shreds with guilt-inducing statements like 'You'll be sorry when I'm dead that you didn't appreciate me' and 'I thought you cared about my life,' I have not heard from him. I've sent him cards on holidays, but have resisted the compulsion to call and apologize for setting my first boundary in our relationship. It may turn out to be the last."

Dr. Wright points out that confrontation can take two very different forms.

In an *indirect* confrontation, you express your feelings without actually facing your father. It can mean writing a letter to your father which you read aloud to an empty chair, a tape recorder, or a friend, but don't actually send. Many women find great comfort in simply getting their feelings out in the open in this way.

If you choose a *direct* confrontation, you can do it by letter, phone, or face to face. But in any case, Dr. Wright recommends that you write down what you want to say, listing what you wanted from your father when you were young that you didn't receive, and then what you want from him now.

I find this wise advice. It can protect you, but it can also be an act of kindness toward your father. When my friend Don's daughter wrote to him in an attempt to alert him to misunderstandings from the past, her letter left Don uncertain about how she wanted him to change.

You might also want to think carefully about the possible ways your father could respond, and how you will handle each. He might admit his wrong, and ask forgiveness. But like Janet's father, he might insist you are the guilty party. Or he may, like the father of one of my friends, simply look blank, and say with a shrug, "Well, *if* I did anything wrong, I'm sorry."

Just because you don't come away with an apology doesn't make direct confrontation a wrong choice. Dr. Wright says it's necessary if you are still being abused by your father in any way, or if you are still so controlled by your father that you can't be an individual, or if you live in fear of him. Janet may not have heard from her father since she confronted him, but she has made enormous steps toward healing in the time since, and I believe the confrontation is part of the reason why.

Confrontation may be difficult; it's often not nearly as hard as making a decision to forgive. Because forgiveness comes so slowly to us, it deserves a chapter of consideration of its own! And it's worth thinking about, because forgiveness can mark the end of mourning and the beginning of joy.

◇ 10 ◇

Forgiving:
Your Way to Freedom

A recent census reported that lawyers now outnumber doctors in our country. Americans, it would appear, care more about getting even than we do about getting well.

In a land whose citizens pledge allegiance to "justice for all," it's difficult for mercy and grace to win much of a hearing. Maybe that's why I sometimes get tired of ministerial challenges to forgiveness. When I know I've been wronged, the human side of me wants reconciliation only after I've had revenge.

Marsha had every right to want revenge on her father. Because of him, her life had been twenty-nine years of chaos. Marsha was the result of a short-lived affair between her mother and father, a married man who promised he was ready to leave his wife. Of course, his story changed abruptly when their encounters produced a pregnancy. Frightened and now alone, Marsha's mother decided to give her baby up for adoption. But Marsha's adoptive parents soon divorced, and Marsha was left to endure physical abuse from her adoptive mother and sexual attacks from her mother's boyfriends.

Much later, in an attempt to put together the puzzle pieces of her life, she decided to try to locate her natural father. What she found was an alcoholic dying of liver disease. When she tried to tell him who she was, he looked at her blankly; then he asked her to repeat her mother's name.

"Was that the red-haired lady who came from Toledo?" he asked her. Marsha said no.

"Then, was she short, and lived with her grandmother?" The answer again was negative. He went on to describe a number of other women with whom he'd had affairs, some of whom he knew by name, others whom he didn't. Finally Marsha was able to elicit from him a fuzzy recollection of her mother. But it was obvious her mother had meant nothing to him, and the fact that he had fathered a daughter meant even less.

As I listened to Marsha's story, I found myself wanting to hurt that man as much as his daughter had been hurt. And more. To consider forgiving him, and challenging Marsha to forgive him, seemed absolutely ridiculous, and almost cruel.

Yet, forgiving her father is just what Jesus would have Marsha do. Why? Because He would have her be free, and His place of freedom can only be entered through the door of forgiveness.

The Opposite of Forgiveness Is . . .

When we've been wronged, we often think we have one of two responses from which to choose. We can either make the positive choice of forgiving the offender, or we can slip into neutral, and idle for a while in the purgatory of unforgiveness. If we don't forgive, we don't see ourselves as evil people, but simply people who've been so deeply wounded we can't forgive just yet.

This picture may be comfortable, but it isn't right. The opposite of forgiveness is not unforgiveness—it is *bitterness*. If we choose not to forgive those who wrong us, we're actually making a definite decision to move in the negative direction of bitterness. There is no purgatory in between. Bitterness can begin from an almost imperceptible start, like a tiny malignant lump in the breast, but it doesn't take much to grow and spread into a cancer that will destroy your life. Bitterness is a particularly lethal option for several terrible reasons.

Bitterness locks Christ out.

Christian counselor Tom Marshall puts it this way: "While we are holding on to bitterness against those who have hurt us, we effectively lock Christ out of the situation. He cannot come in and heal us, no matter how much we ask Him. Forgiveness is an essential prerequisite to healing."[1]

A glass full of water cannot at the same time be full of air. So it is with Christ and bitterness. They cannot co-exist in the same situation, because Christ is Healer. His passion is to move us toward reconciliation and wholeness. It is for these His power exists, since these are the things that bring glory to the Father and peace to His children. The Destroyer, Satan, is the lord of bitterness. So when we choose that bitterness will rule in a relationship, Satan rules as well.

Bitterness keeps you stuck to the one you hate.

Bitterness does more than block our healing. It also keeps us under our abuser's power. Elvin Semrod, teacher

---

[1] Tom Marshall, *Free Indeed* (Auckland, New Zealand: Orama Christian Fellowship Trust, 1983), 54, 55.

of hundreds of Boston psychiatrists, observed: "As long as people are mad at each other, they can't let each other go. As long as [fathers and daughters] don't admit this, as long as they 'hate' each other, they stick together like glue."[2]

I know a woman whose father abused her emotionally for years. She told me, "Only his death will free me from him." But when he dies, she is going to make an unhappy discovery. His death will offer her no relief. She'll be bound to him as long as she is angry, because hatred is as steadfast an emotional bond as is love.

Bitterness turns you into a wound-inflicter.

Paul gives this warning to the Hebrews: "See to it that no one misses the grace of God and no bitter root grows up to cause trouble and defile many" (Hebrews 12:15). Our bitterness will not only harm us but those we love as well.

I saw this principle at work in the life of a woman who believed she simply could not forgive her father for the damage he had done to her life. And to be honest, if it weren't for what I knew about God's imperative to forgive, I would have had to agree with her. The wounds caused by his abuse and neglect came very near to costing her sanity, and her marriage.

But I see, too, that in choosing unforgiveness, she is teaching her children that not every wrongdoing is forgivable. There is an unpardonable sin, and she's defined it as parental abuse. This year, however, her high school age son has decided he's been abused, as well. Not in the horrific ways his mother was, of course, but he can tick off a list of ways his mother's parenting fell short of the ideal. (And what child couldn't?)

The kicker is, he feels a right to harbor bitterness toward her, because in their household, parental abuse was

---

[2]Dr. William Appleton, *Fathers and Daughters* (New York: Doubleday, 1981), 179.

deemed unpardonable. His mother's seed of bitterness is taking root in him, and the wounded one is now seen by her own child as a wounder.

Bitterness stands in the way of rebuilding a new relationship as an adult.

In the twenty, or thirty, or forty years since you and I have grown into adulthood, our fathers have been changing as well. Now that you're no longer a child, there is potential for a new relationship with your father.

Both my mother and stepmother have died in the last twenty years, and those two losses have softened my dad. He's understandably more tender and open than he was during my girlhood. And during those same twenty years, I've developed confidence and life experience I didn't have as a child. So I bring communication skills and understanding to our relationship that I didn't have before.

We can start again. Twenty years ago I didn't know how to say, "When you don't show an interest in my success, I feel . . ." I wasn't mature enough to understand how much he needs my interest in *his* success.

The result of this "starting again" may not be the deepest and most significant communication I'll ever know. As an adult, I see that if my dad hadn't been my dad, if I simply met him at church or at work, we probably wouldn't have chosen each other as best friends, so the depth of our sharing will always be somewhat limited. But that's all right! Because I'm an adult, I have other relational resources on which to draw for intimacy. And because I don't expect him to be everything to me, I can enjoy him for who he is, and appreciate what he's done for me.

But bitterness won't allow a second chance to build a relationship. It allows God no room to maneuver.

The only way to begin to find release from bitterness we feel is by forgiveness. Because our fathers deserve it?

No. We must forgive them because forgiveness is the only way we can find peace. And we can forgive them only as we begin to understand how God forgives *us*.

We Forgive As We Have Been Forgiven

Peter came to Jesus with a question. "How many times shall I forgive my brother when he sins against me? Up to seven times?" Peter probably congratulated himself smugly on his virtue in suggesting such bounteous forgiveness.

But Jesus cut right through his paltry concept of grace. Not seven times, Jesus told him, but seventy-seven! His hearers must have been stunned. Forgive an offender seventy-seven times? Why, even the rabbis required forgiving only three times. Why would Jesus make such an incredible demand?

As if He read their minds, Jesus went on to answer their objections with a story of a king who wanted to bring his accounts up-to-date. To that end, he confronted a slave who owed him ten million dollars. When the slave couldn't pay, the king forgave him, yet the slave refused to forgive another who owed him a lesser amount of money. (See Matthew 18:21–35.)

The lessons from this confrontation? Don't miss them!

First, God is forgiving. He is wildly, ridiculously, incredibly forgiving!

In Jesus' parable, the Master chose to forgive the guilty slave's massive indebtedness. There were no railing accusations. ("How in the world could you have wasted ten million dollars?") There was no reluctant reconciliation. ("I'll write off the debt because there's nothing else I can do, but I intend to remind you every day of your life about your guilt in squandering my money, and how unworthy you are of my kindness.") And He didn't just extend the due date on the debt. ("I'll give you an extra year to come up with the money.")

The Master simply assessed the situation justly. ("You owe me ten million dollars and deserve prison for failing to repay it.") Then He chose to override justice, and instead responded to the servant's plea with a pardon.

It's interesting that Jesus made no mention of the servant being of particularly good character, or especially deserving of forgiveness. The Master chose to forgive because He was being true to His merciful nature. All He wanted in return for His kindness was that the forgiven slave in turn be gracious to others.

As He described this Master, Jesus was, of course, actually unveiling the forgiving nature of His heavenly Father. Just as this good Master forgave his servant, God has graciously chosen to forgive and wash away all our sins.

Have you reveled in the Father's forgiveness for your wrongs? Have you let the immensity of what He has done in washing away your rebellion and disobedience grab hold of you? Have you celebrated the joy of being chosen as His friend, His daughter, His delight?

We won't forgive if we don't know how totally and unconditionally we've been forgiven by God.

Second, because we've been forgiven everything, we can forgive anything.

If we refuse to grant forgiveness, then we have set ourselves up as God, nothing less. We've mandated our own set of requirements for granting forgiveness, even though those requirements differ from God's. He decrees, "If we confess our sins, he is faithful and just and will forgive us our sins" (1 John 1:9). But we go Him one better, and say, "Only if you act sorry enough, or apologize profusely enough, or do enough to make up to me for the pain you've caused . . . only then will I forgive you. And maybe not even then."

If we claim God's "amazing grace" to cover *our* sins, then we have no choice but to pass on grace to those who've sinned against us.

Third, our refusal to forgive our fathers will limit our ability to receive God's forgiveness.

The forgiven servant must have thought his cruelty toward his debtor would have no effect on his relationship to his master. In the same way, we think we can hang on to our "right" to be mad at Dad for what he did to us, yet expect to do this without it having any effect on our relationship to God.

Nothing could be further from reality.

Scripture teaches a mystical, undeniable connection between our heavenly and earthly relationships. "Forgive us our debts," we pray, "*as we forgive our debtors.*" But Jesus followed His model prayer with a stern warning: "If you forgive men when they sin against you, your heavenly Father will also forgive you. But if you do not forgive men their sins, your Father will not forgive your sins" (Matthew 6:14, 15).

Fourth, lack of forgiveness always results in your own misery.

When the unforgiving slave decided to withhold the grace he'd received, he brought endless torture upon himself. It wouldn't take more than ten minutes with any psychologist to come up with a list of the forms these persecutions are taking today. The effects of bitterness and resentment read like a medical text of psychological and physical disorders: broken marriages, loneliness, depression, ulcers and other gastric disorders, arthritis, alienated children, lethargy, obesity—and on and on.

It's not that God decided to inflict these maladies on us as a punishment for unforgiveness. He didn't have to! They follow naturally whenever we choose to block the natural flow of grace that God created our psyches and bodies to pass on to others. He made us to dance in His grace and forgiveness, and then to let that grace overflow from us to those around us. Whenever you and I stop the flow, insisting, "I have a right to be angry!" we do more damage to ourselves than we do to the targets of our anger.

Whatever keeps you from forgiving your father also keeps you from forgiving yourself of your own failings. Nor can you expect others to forgive your failures if you refuse to forgive your father. Nor should you expect to be able to hear answers to your prayers, because as the psalmist explained, "If I had cherished sin in my heart, the Lord would not have listened . . . and heard my prayer" (Psalm 66:18, 19). All these heartaches constitute an enormous price to pay for the "privilege" of nursing a grudge. Forgiving your father is essential to start moving toward healing.

It wasn't until I chose to forgive my father for his short-comings that my eyes opened to another view of him. I resented his lack of willingness to listen and compromise. But I began to see the flip side of this weakness was an ability to stick to his convictions no matter who opposed him.

In contrast, I cower in the face of criticism. It occurred to me that I'd be stronger if I learned from his resolve, and let it become part of me. But I never would have been open to this idea if I had not first chosen forgiveness.

Five Good Arguments Against Forgiving

Maybe you've heard yourself respond with objections like the following:

It's not fair that I have to forgive my father! He made me suffer; justice demands that I make it tough on him! God is just; He promises to punish evil. You don't need to do His work for Him.

But my anger is my strength. If I give it up, I'll collapse in a heap, and my father will walk all over me. Scripture never says our anger is to be our source of strength. It's the joy of the Lord that God intended to be our inner power.

I'll forgive, but first he's got to serve a time of "penance." And meanwhile, you'll be eaten away by the cancer of bitterness.

If I forgive him, what's to keep him from doing it again? He experiences no bad consequences from his wrong if I forgive. What's going to motivate him to change? Since when were you given responsibility to change anyone? It's up to God to change our fathers; our job is simply to respond to what He asks of us.

Forgiveness may mean I have to open my heart to my father. When I've done that before, I've been hurt. What's to keep it from happening again? I need to protect myself from pain. God never intended that you protect yourself, but as long as you try to, He can't help you. Do you fear being a doormat? Scripture says the righteous are bold as lions and as wise as serpents, while still being as innocent as doves. When you stop insisting on protecting yourself, God can teach you this kind of wisdom and strength.

As God's daughter, your self-definition comes from a new dictionary: His Word. No matter how your earthly father responds to you, your heavenly Father says:

> I have loved you with an everlasting love; I have drawn you with loving-kindness. (Jeremiah 31:3)

You are precious and honored in my sight, and . . . I love you. (Isaiah 43:4)

The Lord delights in you and will claim you as his own. (Isaiah 62:4)

Because of what Christ has done we have become gifts to God that he delights in. (Ephesians 1:11)

Because your heavenly Father is the source of all truth, His evaluation of you is the only accurate one. So even if your father ridicules you, you don't have to feel worthless. You can return to what your real Father believes about you, and draw strength from Him to go on toward wholeness.

Forgiving When You're Still in Pain

It's difficult to talk lightly about forgiveness when I think of Mary, whose alcoholic father used to hug the dog and kick his daughter around. Even though Mary may understand the necessity of forgiving her father, she most certainly has a legitimate question when she asks, "How can I forgive when I hurt so much?"

One approach is sure to fail. If we were to try to minimize Mary's pain with bromides like, "At least he didn't throw you out," we'd wind up only increasing her hurt, because she'd be left with a wound, and now guilt that she felt wounded. Trying to convince her that her mountain of pain is actually a molehill is not Jesus' approach. But I can think of two provisions God makes available to those of us who want to forgive.

His power is available.

Some elements of the New Age movement and some pop psychologists have decided forgiveness sounds like a good idea, and have taken it on as one of their "techniques" to move toward wholeness. But when you read their literature, you come away with the idea that forgiveness is something you can do on your own. Just say you've released your offender and *zap!* it's done.

But this kind of "self-help" smells suspiciously like the apostle Paul's description of people who have a form of godliness, but deny its power (2 Timothy 3:5). And he declared them evil.

Real forgiveness is an act of bestowing God's grace upon another, and we can't genuinely minister His grace without calling on His power to do it.

If it seems impossible to forgive your father, that's no problem for God! If it wasn't impossible, you'd try to do it on your own strength. But since it seems impossible to you, you'll need God's help to get the job done. Our God specializes in the impossible. He does His best work when the job can't be done. Remember the parting of the Red Sea? And Christ walking on the water? And the raising of Lazarus from the dead? He's ready to aid us when we finally admit: "With men it is impossible; but with God all things are possible."

Call on His power to help you forgive your father. This One who is reconciling a rotten, rebellious world to His perfect holiness can certainly help you to free you from bitterness and resentment toward your father.

Christ knows how deeply you hurt, and how difficult it is to forgive. But remember, He pardoned those who nailed Him to the cross, even though they never admitted their wrongdoing. You can call on His power to help you forgive, as well.

Forgiveness may be either an event or a journey.

Sometimes forgiveness comes in one magnificent, shining moment that ends the conflict for life. But more often, we have to invoke the "Seventy-seven Principle" Jesus laid down for Peter. In other words, if you've forgiven your father for his wrongdoing, yet the next day you feel the bitterness boiling in you again, it's perfectly all right to forgive him again. And again. And again. Until that stir of bitterness is dead for good. The prison of bitterness can be dismantled by one huge dynamite blast, or it can come down a brick at a time.

We can make forgiveness a habit by practicing it, just as we got better and better at resentment as we practiced it.

Honoring a Dishonorable Father

For some of us, following God's command to honor our fathers comes easily. We don't have to work hard at treating them with respect because they've won our respect by their integrity and love for us. But what about honoring your father if he doesn't seem deserving of honor?

As collegiate counselor Elva McAllaster explains, the verb in this command is simply "to honor."[3] It doesn't say you have to like, or love, or trust him, or even to *feel* respectful toward him. Honoring our fathers means simply treating them with respect.

Maybe for you respectful behavior will mean choosing to stop talking about his faults, even to yourself. Maybe it will mean thanking God for him, weaknesses and all. Maybe it will mean taking initiatives toward him rather than ignoring him.

What we do matters less than that we cultivate an attitude of respect, if not for the man himself, then for the position God has given him. We can ask for—and rely

---

[3] Elva McAllaster's book, *When a Father Is Hard to Honor* (Elgin, Ill.: Brethren Press, 1984), explores the issue of honoring the dishonorable father. Though her book is written to young men, her thoughtful and scriptural approach has wide application for females, as well.

on—God's help in this sometimes difficult task if we do it to honor Him.

Sometimes our initiatives change our fathers for the better. But if they don't change, God's instruction from Romans 12:17–21 has a message for us:

> Do not repay anyone evil for evil. . . . If it is possible, *as far as it depends on you,* live at peace with everyone. Do not be overcome by evil, but overcome evil with good.

God does not hold us responsible to force a reconciliation with our fathers. Some fathers will refuse to admit wrong, or to receive love, so God knows we can only do our part to love them and live peacefully with them. But we can save *ourselves* from evil by thinking good, and doing good toward our fathers, and honoring them for the sake of our heavenly Father's glory.

A Daughter Test

You've had several chances to evaluate your father for places he needs forgiveness. It's just as important to look at how you did as a daughter. You may be standing in need of forgiveness yourself—either from God, or from your father, or from both. So, how about it? How would you answer the following questions?

1. How did you respond when your father didn't live up to your expectations? Was God pleased with your responses?

2. How completely have you obeyed God's command to honor your father?

3. Are there times when you haven't been grateful for what your father has done for you?

4. Have you ever said, "I'll never forgive Dad for that"? Have you since forgiven him, or do you still harbor bitterness?

God pointed out to me my need for repentance at a Christian retreat two years ago. I was in the throes of the father-struggle then, heavy with pain from realizing my dad's lack of involvement, and not yet able to grab on to hope for healing. I could see his faults clearly, but didn't seem able to move beyond them.

After an evening meeting, I stopped a pastor/friend and asked if he would pray with me about the stalemate I felt. As we got ready to pray, I told him a little of my family history.

He was quiet for a moment, then said, "Maybe the Lord has some perspective to offer you so we'll know better how to pray. Could you close your eyes and try to mentally go back to when you were about ten years old, and picture a scene in your home with your family present?"

His request surprised me, but I fixed a family scene in my mind and described it to him. How easy it was to see all of us in the living room with the television on, my dad settled in the big black recliner, my sister and two brothers and me sprawled on the floor or the sofa, mixing homework and television and fussing at each other. Mom wasn't there. She was in the kitchen cutting up apples, it seemed to me. (How amazing these memories of ours must be, to carefully tuck away these scenes from decades ago in such detail!)

With the scene in mind, the pastor then asked me to think of myself in a place alone in the house where I felt safe and comfortable, and I chose my bedroom. "Now," he said, "think of Christ coming to you. Ask Him to help you resolve the distance you feel from your father, and then listen to what He tells you."

Though I heard no audible voice, the thoughts that came to me were these, "Maureen, I wanted to help, but I couldn't, because years ago you decided to protect *yourself* by withdrawing emotionally."

I didn't recall consciously making such a decision, but as I thought about this perspective, it seemed clear that withdrawing was just what I'd done. It also seemed clear that I needed to repent for refusing to let Christ come into the situation. So in the prayer that followed, I did repent and seek God's forgiveness for not trusting Him, and allowing Him to help me.

Those moments broke the stalemate I'd been feeling, and I went home from the retreat with a fresh sense of hope for reconciliation and healing.

Forgiveness does that, of course—opening the way for cleansing and new hope. And we can experience these results whether we are the forgiver, or the one in need of forgiveness, or both.

The psalmist says, "You turned my wailing into dancing; you removed my sackcloth and clothed me with joy" (Psalm 30:11). I believe removing our sackcloth happens as we finish the work of grief by forgiving. And we put on joy when we begin to look beyond our earthly fathers toward our Father in heaven.

◇ 11 ◇

Spiritual Parenting

W hen you and I came to Christ, we gained more than eternal life. We also were born into an enormous, wonderful family. With the help of God's family, it is possible to go back and start over emotionally. Within the family circle of believers, God can begin to fill fathering gaps as He shows us His father care through other believers serving as spiritual fathers.

Popular Bible teacher Josh McDowell, himself the son of an abusive, alcoholic father, says this about God's provision of spiritual fathers:

"God's plan for healing unhealthy self-images and personalities is patterned after his original parenting process. This growth process is a *reparenting*, as spiritual and emotional needs that were not met by relationships with your human parents are now met by God—*through members of the body of Christ*" (emphasis mine).[1]

Dr. Trobisch first made me aware of God's provision for reparenting. He said of his own mother, "She lost her

---

[1]Josh McDowell, *His Image . . . My Image* (Wheaton, Ill.: Tyndale House, 1985), 33–34.

father when she was sixteen. But she had many spiritual fathers. I believe she is a great woman; she knows her womanhood. But she couldn't have without these fathers.

"Not that she couldn't transfer her need [for fathering] after a while to a relationship with her Father God, but we are the body of Christ. We are His feet, His extended hands. That's why I think there needs to be more fathers today who are extending the arms of this loving Father."

Father-Love Is All Around You

Sometimes what we want the most is right within our grasp, but we don't value it. Because if it isn't packaged as we want, we refuse to receive it. The Jews couldn't receive Jesus as their Messiah because they wanted God to come as a conquering king, not a humble servant.

This refusal to receive love can happen to daughters as well. It's easy to feel that unless we get what we need from some person we're fixed on (our dad, for instance, or even a surrogate father), we haven't received at all.

The issue is really one of value. If God chooses to give His parental care through someone other than our biological father, yet we refuse to receive those other sources of love, we're saying God's gifts to us are of no value. On the other hand, we show that we do value His gifts and the giver when we choose to receive care from anyone offering it, even if the giver wasn't the one we'd hoped for.

My friend Traci showed me how this works. In her Christmas letter, she talked about the joy she was finding in being part of what she called her "family of choice." The traumas of Traci's biological family could make a good television mini-series, but instead of choosing a lifetime of wallowing in what might have been, Traci has chosen to receive God's love where she *does* find it—in the people she's aptly named her "family of choice."

Maybe you don't resist the *idea* of being reparented, but perhaps you are not profiting from messages of love and leadership God is offering through spiritual fathers *because you won't believe them.* This can be another way of devaluing God's gift.

Joe Aldrich, president of Multnomah School of the Bible in Oregon, uses the imagery of a person walking through life carrying two empty buckets. Each time we receive love or positive reinforcement from another, it goes into our buckets. And as they fill, our self-worth increases. But there are those who clamp lids on their buckets so tightly that no positive reinforcement can get in. They've become convinced they are unworthy of love, so when affirmation comes their way, they simply cannot believe it, and their bucket stays empty. But a choice toward faith and away from unbelief is all it takes to begin to pry the bucket open.

Finding your "family of choice" is what spiritual reparenting is all about. When you understand how enthusiastically the Scriptures speak of reparenting, you'll be encouraged in the search. And the Bible offers models, too, to show where to go to create just such a family.

Reparenting in the Scriptures

Paul and Timothy provide a wonderful scriptural model of spiritual fathering at its best. Timothy was born to a pagan Greek father and a godly Hebrew mother. We're never told if his father died early in Timothy's life, or if he simply didn't influence his son significantly. All we know is that his mother Eunice and his grandmother Lois taught him the Scriptures, and after they responded to Paul's preaching, Timothy responded, too.

Later, Timothy joined Paul in his ministry, and Paul

became a father to this young man. Paul called him "my true child in the faith" (1 Timothy 1:2), and, "my beloved son" (2 Timothy 1:2). He taught Timothy the ways of God, and mentored him to a place of effective service. Like a good parent, he instructed, encouraged and challenged Timothy to full maturity as a Christian and a man. And Paul's letters to Timothy are warm with fatherly tenderness. "I constantly remember you in my prayers night and day," he tells the young man, "longing to see you, even as I recall your tears, that I may be filled with joy" (2 Timothy 1:3, 4). The fathering Timothy lacked, God gave him through the apostle Paul, and He can make just such a provision for us today.

Recognizing Spiritual Fathering

One very complete kind of spiritual fathering is the *replacement father.* The Bible illustrates this in the story of Esther. When her parents died, her cousin Mordecai became a replacement father for Esther. He took her into his home, and guided and cared for and launched her into adulthood. And when she grew up, he treated her as a respected peer.

Some girls find their "Mordecai" in genuine father-bonding with a stepfather. My friend Julie found a replacement father in her pastor. Julie lost her father to alcoholism during the most formative years of her female identity. I wondered why she didn't seem to exhibit the scars one would expect.

When I asked her about it, she answered at once, "Daddy drank some when I was little, but for the most part he was loving and fun to be with. It wasn't until I was in junior high that his drinking got bad. But about that time, I started going to a new church. The pastor and his wife took a special interest in me and treated me like their own daughter." Replacement fathering made up for what an earthly father wasn't providing.

Another less complete, but more common, kind of spiritual parenting is the *partial father*. In this type of role, a man may offer some facet of God's paternal care for a limited period of time.

As Laura worked to change her attitude toward her cold and rejecting father, she found a spiritual father in the psychologist who was counseling her. She opened her feelings to this older man and found she could still be accepted, even liked. In a sense, he was used of God for a time to become the warm, accepting, nurturing daddy she never had.

During the same period, Laura worked for a godly man who exhibited another facet of fathering. He encouraged her professionally, praised her and treated her with respect. Together these two men helped to provide her with a healthy model of a caring father.

As she healed, Laura's need for their support lessened, but they were instrumental in filling the vacuum her own father had left when it came to guiding and launching her into adulthood.

Hearing Laura's story made me look back at my life and begin to see places the Lord provided parenting for me through partial fathering.

I thought of my high school Spanish teacher, who had the grace to treat silly and insecure adolescents with respect. He used to address us as "Miss" or "Mister" and would veer our class discussions off into tangents where we'd grapple with real-life issues. And he'd actually consider what we had to say. He taught me I could have ideas that a man I respected would listen to.

The director of our youth group also served as surrogate father for a time. He took an interest in my spiritual growth, and his willingness to offer advice and to include me in his family supplied a fatherly kind of camaraderie that met a need.

And there are many others.

Partial fathering is important to recognize because, most often, God reparents us through a number of His people, not just one. If all our reparenting needs were met through one daddy substitute, the temptation would be great to expect too much from the relationship. We might find ourselves bonding to the man himself, rather than seeing him as God's instrument to bond us to himself.

Cautions About Spiritual Fathers

In her book *When a Father Is Hard to Honor,* Dr. Elva McAllaster offers a caution about what she calls "borrowing" a father.

"To borrow a father can be encouragement and stimulus and solace and reassurance. It can stabilize identity when the turmoils of living have left one's compasses and gyroscopes either out of kilter or mistrusted. It needs common sense, though, lest the borrower lean too hard and place undue demands."[2]

Her reminder about common sense is a good one, and it applies particularly when the borrowers are women, and the lenders men. No matter how well-intentioned and spiritual we are, any time a man meets a woman's deep emotional needs, sexual electricity between them seems inevitable.

Or even if the relationship generates no recognizable sexual energy, it's easy to develop inappropriate expectations of the man God is using in our lives. We can tell ourselves, "He's met this need, so I can expect he'll meet these others as well," and wind up disappointed.

---

[2]Elva McAllaster, *When a Father Is Hard to Honor* (Elgin, Ill.: Brethren Press, 1984), 60–61.

We need to be aware of these dangers and exercise common sense. Laura, whom I mentioned earlier, had spiritual fathers who were both older, mature, happily married men with grown daughters. And both had discretion enough to keep their relationship to her on a warm, but professional level. No invitations to dinner. No private appointments after office hours. And Laura makes it a practice to enjoy the friendship of married men only if she is also close to their wives. Common sense can make the difference between ministry and misery.

And it's been my experience that when I've become inappropriately dependent on a surrogate father, the Lord has often taken him out of my life. I have not always been overjoyed when He's done this, but in the long run I've been very grateful. We need to guard ourselves from evil, and also trust that God will guard us.

Spiritual fathers are a gift from God. Like any gift, it can be misused. But that doesn't mean we should refuse to receive one or more as God's provision.

Receiving Spiritual Fathering

To some women, the idea of receiving help from spiritual fathers doesn't play well. These women insist they'd rather "rely only on the Lord, instead of on men." But God has created all of us—male and female alike—as dependent creatures. We cannot exist in isolation, and we can't grow to maturity in isolation. God himself is a trinity, three interdependent beings that make up a unified whole.

And as women, we need affirming relationships with men to help us discover the true meaning of our femaleness, just as men can never fully grasp their maleness without having it affirmed by females. "In the Lord, neither is woman independent of man, nor is man independent of woman" (1 Corinthians 11:11). Reading this scripture always brings to mind one of my favorite quotes from Madeleine L'Engle's book, *The Irrational Season*: "God promised to make you free. He never promised to make you independent."

As Westerners, we harbor the mistaken notion that maturity insists on independence. And particularly for those who've suffered deep abuse or severe neglect, dependence may feel like becoming a victim again.

One such woman said, "All my adult life ... I had perceived myself to be a rather strong, independent go-getter. Rarely asking help with anything, I was committed not to bother people, not to be in anyone's debt. If something broke, I either fixed it myself or paid someone else to do it. I changed my own oil, fixed my own flat tires, handled the closing on my first home, and dug my own hole when I wanted to plant a tree. I was always in charge. Most often, I was the one to say, 'Don't worry, we'll take my car,' or 'I've got money, so I'll pay for the food.' To allow anyone to inconvenience himself for me seemed the height of presumption."[3]

In God's view, though, true maturity leads to healthy interdependence—trust in Him that allows us to need others, as well as letting them need us. If we only allow a one-sided relationship, wherein we take care of others, then we're controllers, not servants in the biblical sense. Even our Lord, who came "not to be served, but to serve," allowed himself to be dependent. He needed His disciples to go for food, to share their homes, to arrange for their last supper, and pray with Him when He was distressed. Women supported Him financially. Jesus was not His own best friend. He told the disciples, "You are my friends." He let himself be vulnerable.

But in wisdom, He didn't trust everyone with His

---

[3]Lottie K. Hillard, "Overcoming the Shame of Needing: A Journey Toward Becoming a Woman," *IBC Perspective*, vol. 2, 9–19.

deepest self. John 2:23–25 explains this clearly:

> Because of the miracles he did in Jerusalem at the Pass-
> over celebration, many people were convinced that he
> was indeed the Messiah. *But Jesus didn't trust them, for he
> knew mankind to the core. No one needed to tell him how
> changeable human nature is!* (The Living Bible, emphasis
> mine)

He did, however, open His heart to twelve who had given up something to follow Him and be His friends. Sometimes they let Him down—for instance, when Judas betrayed Him, and Peter denied Him, and Thomas doubted Him. But His willingness to risk openness with these twelve also made possible relationships in which some came to love Him enough to die for Him.

Healthy interdependence means not only giving to those who need something from you, but receiving from those who have something to offer you.

If a father affirms his daughter as person and woman, he's given her an unspeakable gift. But if he fails, God has other servants through whom He can offer this needed affirmation. Jesus promised, "Everyone who has left . . . father . . . for my sake will receive a hundred times as much and will inherit eternal life" (Matthew 19:29). These are the spiritual fathers of which the Scriptures speak. We need to recognize them, give thanks for them, and allow God to use them to help us understand His father-love for us.

My Father Becomes a Spiritual Father As Well

I've written earlier about how emotionally distant from my father I felt growing up, and some of the implications those feelings had for my adult life.

But as I made some of the discoveries I've shared with

you—about the need to look back, to mourn, to forgive, and to receive reparenting—I saw my attitude toward my father change from one of disappointment and fear to acceptance and respect. I doubt if outsiders would have noticed any difference in our behavior when we were together, but I knew I was freer to love and honor him because I no longer so desperately hungered for his approval. For this healing, I felt glad and grateful.

But in this year, our story has taken an interesting twist.

A year ago, my husband and I moved our family into a new home we had just built. What should have been a dream come true turned into a nightmare when it looked as if massive differences with our builder might keep us from owning the home, after all. For various reasons, it fell to me to confront the builder about these differences, while fully expecting he'd refuse to budge. I knew I'd need support, and my husband suggested I talk it over with my dad. So I did.

I packed up all the paperwork and went to his house. While we finished off a pot of coffee, I explained the whole mess as best I could.

He helped me decide where we'd gone wrong, and to come up with a plan to present to the builder. Then we worked on alternatives, in case our plan wasn't accepted. He did include a gentle admonition, "Well," he said, "you kids probably didn't handle this as wisely as you could have, but I know you're learning for next time." Otherwise there was no criticism. As a good father, he simply helped *me* figure a way out, then encouraged me that I could do it.

I did resolve the problems. His suggestions were right. And though the confrontation with our builder scared me silly, it calmed me to know my dad was behind me. And when it was done, Dad told me I did well . . . then bought us two beautiful storm doors for the new house to celebrate!

In this "second chance" for us, I realize I'm more fortunate than many daughters. For one thing, my dad lived long enough to be able to re-do some of the past. And the pain of my mother and stepmother's deaths has mellowed him from what he was when I was a girl. And he knows Christ, so he's had the Holy Spirit's influence to move him toward positive change.

Of course, not everything is different. If I'd come to him with an emotional problem rather than a business-related one, he might not have been able to give like he did. And he still gives a storm door to say "I love you" instead of giving a hug. Everything isn't different, but what *is* different is wonderful! And it's filling a father-void in me.

Living With a Father Who Won't Change

If your story doesn't appear to be ending as satisfyingly as has mine, if your father continues to cause you pain, what then? How do you behave toward a father who gives you grief?

Here it's helpful to remember God has given us "a spirit of power, and love, and a sound mind" (2 Timothy 1:7). His power in us means we can control our initiatives toward a difficult father; we can behave in a loving way. And we can control our responses to him; we can make sound decisions about responding maturely. Our father no longer needs to control us by his anger, or blaming, or distance, or intimidation.

Being in control of yourself means you can choose to behave as a loving and honoring daughter should. You can send birthday and Father's Day cards whether he does or not. You can keep your father up-to-date on your life, whether he seems to care or not. You can look for ways to praise and thank him, both in his presence and to others, even if he never praises you. You can ask for advice in fields where he's knowledgeable, even if he doesn't recognize the graciousness and maturity you've shown in asking.

And you can speak truth to him when he hurts you. Collegiate counselor Dr. Elva McAllaster says, "After a traumatic weekend at home, can you write a calm letter telling Dad that you really must tell him it makes you very angry for him to—to—to what? (What does he do?) To pummel you with advice you haven't asked for? To make decisions for you willy-nilly?"

But she adds, "I'm not suggesting the kind of enlightenment that would yell at him in accusations, invective and sweeping shrill cries of 'You always . . .' and 'You never. . . .' Yet even a thunderstorm like that might clear away a good many clouds eventually. It might be better than anger that grows and struggles and writhes inside you."[4]

To take either one of these initiatives, praising or rebuking, may require the support of a mediator. When you're with your father, you may need a friend or your husband along. I'm thinking of someone who will help see him through different eyes, and can help you sort out what is praiseworthy in him from what can rightly be confronted.

Beyond these actions, though, cultivating an attitude of grace is what makes relating to a continually hurtful father easier. The very word "hurtful," after all, comes from the phrase "full of hurt." Our dads may continue to wound because they themselves have been wounded. Have you ever thought of your father as a baby? As a child?

---

[4]McAllaster, 115–116.

A young husband? Who was he to *his* parents? To his brothers and sisters? What did he want from life?

One afternoon with my dad's ninety-year-old sister gave me a whole new way of seeing my father. Dad never said much about growing up, except that his father died when he was nine. But Aunt Helen filled in that sketchy outline with the relational dynamics in that fatherless household which shaped my dad's adult behavior. For me, understanding helped turn blaming to empathy.

It helps us to find what my friend and editor David Hazard calls "a pocket of grace" in our hearts in which to place our father's failings. And with these failings covered by the grace of Christ—the same grace that covers *our* sins—we have a resource from which to make clearer, healthier, and wiser decisions about how to relate to fathers who can't, or won't, give.

Coming Full Circle

God's father-care is everywhere. We can find our father hunger lessening as we learn to hear His words of love and recognize His provision of spiritual fathering. Then, as daughters whose emotional tanks are being refilled, we can in turn give to our earthly fathers the love and honor God intended for them.

◇ 12 ◇

The Father-God Connection

How would you complete the following sentence? When I was growing up, my father was _____ to me.

When I think of my heavenly Father, the first picture that comes to mind is _____ .

Ruth answered this way: "When I was growing up, my father was a strong, steady, positive *authority* to me." Then she went on to say , "When I think of my heavenly Father, the first picture that comes to my mind is my need to lovingly and consistently *obey* His will for my life."

Diane, on the other hand, described her father as "distant and uninvolved." When she thinks of God, she admits, "I struggle continually with the concept of a heavenly Father who wants a close relationship with me."

Diane's conflicts may mirror those of a friend of mine who wrote this poem:

She was shelling peas,
apron-covered knees
spread wide to catch
each pea/each pod.

134

I, shaky, needy,
wandered near.

Her ancient swollen hands
pushed back the hair
that hid my face.

She set down the pan and,
patting her knee,
said:

Oh, child,
come on up here
and let me have a look at you.

Her voice was safe and so was I,
sitting in the lap of God.[1]

Maybe you wouldn't go as far as insisting that God be called "Mother," but the point is this: Though we know all the Bible verses about God's fatherly care, many of us live like spiritual and emotional orphans, begging other starving orphans to drop a coin in our empty cup as if we're totally unaware that we have a Father who is alive and well and aching to care for us. Why is this so?

Dr. Bruce Narramore answers:

My experience in counseling neurotic adults has invariably shown that their image of God has been colored by negative experiences with parents, God's representatives on earth. This is not to say that biblical teachings on God's character fail to influence our spiritual relationships. They certainly do. *But negative emotional reactions stemming from childhood interfere with our ability to apply biblical knowledge.*[2]

A study by Daniel Trobisch, then a doctoral student at

---

[1]Martha Popson, "The Lap of God," *Daughters of Sarah* (November/December 1987), 19.
[2]Bruce Narramore, *Help! I'm a Parent!* (Grand Rapids, Mich.: Zondervan Publishing House, 1972), 13–14.

the University of Salzberg in Austria, supports Dr. Narramore's conclusion. Two influences had led to Daniel Trobisch's interest in fathers of daughters. The first grew out of a counseling-by-correspondence ministry he shared with his father, Dr. Walter Trobisch. As the two answered letters from teenage girls, Daniel Trobisch was impressed with how many of those with personality or relationship problems also reported poor relationships with their fathers.

About this same time, he came across a study analyzing prostitutes in the redlight district in Hamburg. The study noted that a large percentage of the women had disrupted relationships with their fathers. This observation, coupled with what he had seen in the young women he counseled, peaked his interest.

How does a father affect his daughter, particularly as she views God the Father? Through in-depth interviews with thirty German women, Trobisch probed the image each had of her earthly father, and then tested to uncover her picture of God. Dr. Trobisch found that *every woman* in his study saw God with the same characteristics she observed in her father.

In God's design, our earthly fathers were to begin the task of introducing us to our heavenly Father. And its not by accident God chose to describe himself with the same word that identifies our earthly dads.

Biologically speaking, every human being has a father, or they'd never have appeared on this planet. Not everyone on earth has to have a king to exist, but our fathers are essential for life itself. So it is with God.

And each of has only one father. An ovum can't be fertilized by two different sperm at the same instant and still go on to a live birth. In the same way, our spiritual life comes, not from many gods—just One.

A father is necessary to our lives, and his position is

unique. So God is essential to our spiritual existence. He is unique, the only God. But God gave us men to father us for relational reasons, as well.

These men were to teach us God's father-nature from Scripture, and help us recognize and respond to Christ's work in our lives. God intended our fathers show us what His embrace feels like when He loves us, what His voice sounds like when He corrects us, what His smile looks like as He delights in us.

Earthly relationships were given to model heavenly ones. The Scriptures make this clear in a number of places, but two passages illustrate it especially well:

> What of you, if his son asks for bread, will give him a stone? Or if he asks for a fish, give him a snake? If you, then, though you are evil, know how to give good gifts to your children, how much more will your Father in heaven give good gifts to those who ask Him! (Matthew 7:9–11)

When Jesus wanted His listeners to understand God's generosity and grace, He used an earthly father's care to point the way to God.

> We have all had human [earthly] fathers who disciplined us and we respected them for it. How much more should we submit to the Father of our spirits and live! Our fathers disciplined us for a little while as they thought best; but God disciplines us for our good, that we may share in his holiness. (Hebrews 12:9–10)

How are we to understand God's discipline? By thinking of our fathers' correction, of course, and using it to point us to lessons of God.

God knew some of those reading His Word would enjoy godly fathering; others would suffer under abysmal fathering; and most would experience a mix of both good and bad. Fathers who abandon and abuse and ignore their children aren't a phenomenon exclusive to the twentieth century. But that didn't deter God from admonishing His people to look to their earthly parenting experiences to learn heavenly lessons. Sometimes we learn by positive example, other times by seeing what God is *not* like. But either way, Scripture boldly encourages believers to think about the example of their earthly fathers as they seek union with the heavenly Father.

Your Own Father-God Connection

It's tough to be objective about the people in our lives who matter most to us. I've found helpful a simple tool which can help women evaluate for themselves their emotional portrait of both God and their fathers. This instrument was designed by Dr. Bruce Narramore.

So take the next few minutes and answer the questions that follow—first as they describe your relationship to your father, then your relationship to God. Don't work too hard at being sure your answer is perfect. Instead, go with your first reaction, and put a check by the statement that most nearly describes your feelings.

Dr. Narramore includes a warning that you need to heed as you answer. He says: "Those of us without serious emotional problems often experience a 'halo effect.' On exercises like this we tend to mark most items above average. We choose our answers on the basis of what we think [they] should be, or on the basis of our intellectual reasoning. For this exercise to be helpful, you must answer with your *feelings,* not with your *thoughts.* For example, we all 'know' God loves us. But most of us have times when we don't 'feel' his love. Select your answers according to your feelings."[3]

---

[3]Bruce Narramore, *A Guide to Child-Rearing* (Grand Rapids, Mich.: Zondervan, 1972), 41–42.

And just as you did when you took the Fathering Inventory, it will help to give yourself a moment or two of quiet before you begin. You've just been doing a very cognitive activity—reading—and now I'm asking you to answer with your feelings. That transition may take a little time. Now, go on and choose the answers which best fit you.

How I Saw My Father

Communication:

1. Rarely had good communication
2. Communicated, but often on a superficial level
3. Communicated frequently and meaningfully

Emotional Warmth:

1. Cold and distant
2. Slightly cold and distant
3. Cordial, but not very warm
4. Moderately warm and close
5. Very warm and close

Discipline:

1. Lax and insufficient
2. Firm, but sometimes harsh or inconsistent
3. Firm but loving
4. Overly strict
5. Moderate controls based on mutual respect

Acceptance:

1. Felt continually rejected
2. Felt accepted only when performance was good
3. Usually felt accepted
4. Continually felt accepted

Father's Satisfaction With Performance:

1. Rarely pleased with me
2. Occasionally pleased with me
3. Often pleased with me
4. Nearly always pleased with me

Father's Emotional Outlook:

1. Always optimistic and happy
2. Usually optimistic and happy
3. Often moody and depressed
4. Usually depressed and moody

How I See God

Communication:

1. Rarely have good communication through prayer or Bible study
2. Communicate, but often on a superficial level
3. Communicate frequently and meaningfully

Emotional Relationship With God:

1. Seems very cold and distant
2. Slightly cold and distant
3. Cordial, but not warm
4. Moderately warm and close
5. Very warm and close

Feeling Toward God's Discipline:

1. Seems insufficient
2. Seems firm, but sometimes harsh and inconsistent
3. Seems firm but loving
4. Seems harsh at times
5. Seems adequate and appears to be based on respect

Feelings About God's Acceptance:

1. Feel continually rejected
2. Feel accepted only when I perform
3. Usually feel accepted
4. Always feel accepted

God's Emotional Attitude:

1. Feel God is often angry with me
2. Feel God is occasionally upset with me
3. Feel God is disappointed with me
4. Feel God is satisfied with me

Can you see correlations between your image of God and your feelings toward your father? Some women do, but others don't as easily. One reason might be that not every kind of inadequate fathering results in the same kind of response to God.

In his counseling of sexually abused women, psychologist John Musser has observed wounded women exhibiting two different reactions toward God. Some take the approach you might expect. They say, "God? I hate Him! He's just like all men."

But other women take a "God-is-so-holy-and-I'm-so-hopelessly-sinful" attitude. This stance makes sense when you understand that many women who've been sexually abused feel terribly guilty, as if somehow they must have been responsible for what was done to them. Or even if they don't carry the burden of responsibility, they may harbor a deep sense of shame and worthlessness.

So one abused woman sees God as vindictive and cruel; another might describe Him as perfect and untouchable. But both have drawn their false conclusions from the well of deficit fathering.

Six Struggles With the Character of God

A leader in an international organization watched his father walk out of their home, never to return. At age ten, he felt shattered. The years ahead brought a succession of stepfathers, some kind, others remembered as "weird." After he became a Christian, his path to faith in God's character was littered with boulder-sized obstacles left in the aftermath of his parents' divorce. His experiences have helped him define the problem areas that often plague those who had less than adequate fathering when they came to Christ.

The solution to each of these problems lies in Paul's admonition to "fight the good fight of the faith" (1 Timothy 6:12). We fight against lies about God's character by choosing to believe instead what He's said in His Word, whether we feel like it or not. Looking at the places where our fathers have mis-instructed us about God can help us know where we particularly need to let God speak for himself:

You may have trouble believing God will never abandon you.

The young man mentioned previously recalled thinking after his father's departure: "Just about the time you need your dad to be there, he'll split." For women who've experienced a similar disappointment, it may be difficult to expect God to act differently.

Yet God says, "Can a mother forget the baby at her breast and have no compassion on the child she has borne? Though she may forget, I will not forget you! See, I have engraved you on the palms of my hands" (Isaiah 49:15, 16).

You may struggle against God's authority.

How do you respond when God tells you to do this or that? Do you obey right away, or wait until He's repeated His command ten or fifteen times? Does He have to shout at you to get you to obey?

If He does, you may be responding to Him as you did to your passive or distant father.

Or else you may jump when you hear His command, but you may have trouble believing that when He corrects you He still loves you.

But your heavenly Father has only good intentions when He directs or disciplines you. " 'For I know the plans I have for you,' declares the Lord, 'plans to prosper you and not to harm you, plans to give you hope and a future' " (Jeremiah 29:11).

You may not believe God wants to give to you.

If your father didn't give, or gave grudgingly, or wrapped each of his gifts in reminders of how much he'd done for you and how little you'd done for him, you learned little from him of God's generosity. Receiving from God may be difficult for you because you can't believe He wants to give to you.

Yet Paul reminds us, "He who did not spare his own Son, but gave him up for us all—how will he not also, along with him, graciously give us all things?" (Romans 8:32).

Loving and being loved by God may be difficult.

If you ever came with open arms to your father but he didn't respond, you may be reluctant to express affection to God. You know you ought to. But emotionally you may fear loving God because you expect that your love isn't welcomed or reciprocated.

Impossible! "God demonstrates his own love for us in this: While we were still sinners, Christ died for us" (Romans 5:8). Jesus, with His arms outstretched on the cross, is God offering you His embrace. And when you return His love, this is the response you'll find: "He will rejoice over you in great gladness; he will love you and not accuse you." Then the Old Testament writer pauses to hear the sound of singing, and he exclaims, "Is that a joyous choir I hear? No, it is the Lord himself exulting over you in happy song" (Zephaniah 3:17, TLB). Your love for God makes heaven sing!

You may not feel confident in God's faithfulness.

When a dad says, "Saturday we're going on a picnic," and there's no picnic when Saturday rolls around, a daughter learns her father's word means nothing. He'll keep his promises if it's convenient, or if he remembers, or if nothing else comes up. She'll likely expect God to behave the same way.

But He can't, because "as for God, his way is perfect; the word of the Lord is flawless" (Psalm 18:30). He's not reluctant to make it clear *His* word can be trusted. He declares:

> I publicly proclaim bold promises; I do not whisper obscurities in some dark corner so that no one can know what I mean. And I didn't tell Israel to ask me for what I didn't plan to give! No, for I, Jehovah, speak only truth and righteousness." (Isaiah 45:19, TLB)

Sharing your heart with God may not come easily.

It had been a tough day for eleven-year-old Nancy. The geography test she expected to ace came back with a red "F" because she'd misunderstood the directions. When Nancy dragged in the back door, she was more than ready to spill her misery to her dad. And he did well at listening, until Nancy began to cry. Her dad pulled away, and delivered a stern lecture about how Nancy shouldn't be crying.

Nancy learned from the encounter not to show her emotions to her dad if she wanted to be accepted. Now she counsels her younger sister, "Don't let Daddy see you cry."

What does this "lesson" do to Nancy's relationship with God? She may begin to edit what she tells Him, so her prayers sound "spiritual enough" to please Him. Prayers need to be sterilized and passionless, or she will again risk the chastisement she felt from her father. But the One to whom she prays demands no such sterility. He would say to her, "Trust in him at all times, O people; pour out your hearts to him, for God is our refuge" (Psalm 62:8).

If her father fails her, a woman can still connect deeply

to God through learning to choose to believe His Word, and through experiencing Christ's work made real to her by members of His family on earth. You'll understand more about these two provisions in the chapters ahead.

◊ 13 ◊

Bonding to Your Heavenly Father

Consider this daughter's Father's Day tribute to her dad.[1]

It's Father's Day, Daddy, and here I sit wrapping your gift, filled with memories about growing up as your daughter. For instance, do you remember that time long ago when I went on my first dinner date? I was pretty young and shy, and still liked horses better than boys. But you encouraged me to get out. You knew I'd have a fine time.

A corsage came that afternoon. I will never forget the way my heart turned over when I lifted it out of the box. You said I must be very special to get flowers. Me—special? I couldn't stop looking at them. I studied myself in the mirror, wishing I were prettier. I had an awful scratch on my nose. But when it was time for me to go, you said I looked beautiful. Those were your very words.

"Don't stay out too late," Mama said, laughing. You smiled, too, and tapped your watch. I was so nervous I

<hr>

[1]Sue Monk Kidd, "Sincerely . . . ," *Guideposts* (June 1988), 45.

slammed the car door on the hem of my dress.

At the restaurant I was sure everybody was staring at me. Hadn't they ever seen two people on a date? Or was it my nose everyone was gazing at? I felt awkward—you know how unsure of myself I was in those days.

The table was just for two, with a candle glowing on it. Conversation was easier than I'd expected. Now that I think about it, I did all the talking. I kept talking right through dessert—about how I wished I could grow up to be a nurse or a writer and travel to Africa to take care of starving children. I was full of dreams back then. They seemed pretty unlikely to me, but that night I talked about them, and somehow started to believe I could do some of those things.

Then when I came back home, I was kissed on the cheek. I wanted to say in return, "Thanks for the corsage and the dinner and for making an uncertain girl feel so special." But none of that came out. All I could say to my date was, "You're too much!" I said it over and over. In the language of a 12-year-old that meant someone was too wonderful for words.

Well, Daddy, I'm almost finished wrapping your gift now. But suddenly it doesn't seem like very much. A shirt. Did I give you a shirt last year too? Why do my gifts at Father's Day always seem so inadequate? Is it because I know deep inside that no matter what I give, you have given me still more?

You gave me confidence in myself twenty-five years ago. How was it you put it? "You can be anything you want to be. Just believe in yourself." That's what you said the night we dined in that restaurant on our one and only "date." And even today, when words don't come, I still say, "You're too much, Daddy!" You really are.

Sue Monk Kidd, who wrote the thank-you just read, enjoyed superb fathering, to be sure. But I have wonderful news. Even if your earthly dad deserved no such glowing tribute, you can still enjoy the care of a father much more wonderful than Sue's.

If you have committed your life to Jesus Christ, you now belong to the Son of God who redeemed you from your sin by His death and resurrection. But at the same time Christ became yours, the Father of the Lord Jesus Christ became your own father. And at that moment, you were fully and freely adopted into His family as His own daughter. *"I will be a Father to you, and you will be my . . . daughters, says the Lord Almighty"* (2 Corinthians 6:18).

Letting Your Heavenly Father Speak for Himself

So how do we go on to grow closer to our heavenly Father? I have three suggestions.

First, give God a chance to speak for himself. Look to *Scripture* to uncover a true portrait of God's fatherly nature and care.

The Bible gives us a clear picture of our Father's character and how He relates to us. We get to know Him accurately as we see Him in His Word, which reverberates with truths like these:

O Lord, you are our Father. We are the clay, you are the potter; we are all the work of your hand. (Isaiah 64:8)

For all who are led by the Spirit of God are [daughters] of God. And so we should not be like cringing, fearful slaves, but we should behave like God's very own children, adopted into the bosom of His family, and calling to Him, "Father, Father." (Romans 8:14–15, TLB)

Listing all the places in Scripture that talk about our heavenly Father would make a book in itself. The New Testament alone speaks of Him as Father over 260 times!

You may be new to the Bible, or new to looking in it

for a specific insight. To help you get started, I've included in the back of this book several of what I believe are the very best passages dealing with God's father love for you. You might want to think about one of these passages each day for the next couple of weeks. If you're more experienced in studying the Bible, you might want to do your own study in the book of John, especially chapters fourteen to sixteen, as Jesus speaks to His disciples at their last supper together. This discourse is peppered with references to God the Father. You could mark each, and then consider what the statement teaches about your Father and what He wants to do for you. In the translation I use, I found forty-two references to the Father, so if you mulled over only two a day, you'd have three weeks of meditations mapped out for you.

But just reading the Bible verses won't impact you. You'll want to read the words aloud, and then ask yourself:

What do I learn about God?

What does He want to do for me?

What is my response?

I have a little notebook where I record the insights I get. My responses vary: Sometimes I say a simple "thank you" for who He is; often I write a prayer in response; sometimes, I think of something He wants me to correct or change in my life.

Once your eyes open to God's fathering in Scripture, you'll see it everywhere. And familiar teaching will take on new meaning as you consider them in light of your Father's character.

For instance, I've often quoted God's promise, "Never will I leave you; never will I forsake you" (Hebrews 13:5). But as I began to seek to know my heavenly Father, I realized that verse told me I have an *involved* Father. He's never absent, either physically or psychologically.

When I think of Jeremiah 31:3, in which the Lord affirms, "I have loved you with an everlasting love; I have drawn you with loving-kindness," it now speaks to me of my Father's *warmth*.

I read: "The Lord disciplines those he loves, as a father the [daughter] he delights in" (Proverbs 3:12). It reminds me my Father isn't passive; He guides and *disciplines* me for my good.

And my Father doesn't try to be too wonderful, and keep me a spiritual child. He *launches* me, as He insists that I "become mature, attaining to the whole measure of the fullness of Christ. Then we will no longer be infants" (Ephesians 4:13, 14a).

The Bible holds the truth about our Father's character and His care. Hearing His words of father-love in Scripture can help us grow close to God.

Second, open your eyes to see His daily, fatherly care.

Our daughter is three weeks away from turning twelve. As Mike and I watch her bouncing out the door to a movie with her friends, or off to her room to *her* music, we're very aware of how close she stands to the threshold of womanhood. And I'm interested to hear my husband thinking aloud about how he wants to help her in the years ahead as she ventures out into a sea of volatile emotions and churning hormones.

As I see his desire to protect and instruct his daughter, my mind goes back to the summer of my fourteenth year when I boarded a bus bound for North Platte, Nebraska, to spend the next five weeks at a Bible camp called Maranatha. During those five weeks, I worked and played and studied and witnessed with a group of high-schoolers and collegians who were immensely serious about God. The camp existed to provide an immersion into what it meant to be Christ's disciple during the 167 hours a week we *weren't* in church. We learned to apply scriptural principles to how we straightened our beds, how we whacked a volleyball, how we treated our cabin mates, and how we made decisions about sexual purity.

Most of the other campers were older than I, which worked greatly to my advantage. Most were well beyond junior-high struggles with puppy love and looking for real answers to their questions about dealing with their emerging sexuality. Consequently, we studied God's plan for marriage and His standards for holiness. I discovered not only God's standards, but I knew the why behind them and what kinds of behaviors would make achieving those standards a reality. Being with those dedicated teenagers raised my sights for what God could give me in a Christian mate and helped me determine not to settle for less.

It occurred to me recently that in sending me to that camp, God had instructed me in the same way Mike wants to instruct our own little girl. That camping experience was God's way of providing the information, motivation, and the attractive modeling I needed to deal with the temptations that lay ahead through high school and college.

Recognizing God's work helps me appreciate the fathering He is continually providing. And it gives me confidence for the future that He will continue to care for me as any good father does his daughter.

Third, we can grow closer to our heavenly Father as we see His ways even through father failures.

Theologian J. I. Packer says this:

> It is just not true in the realm of personal relations that positive concepts cannot be formed by contrast. . . . Many young people get married with a resolve not to make the mess of marriage that they saw their parents make: can this not be a positive ideal? Similarly, the thought of our Maker becoming our perfect parent— faithful in love and care, generous and thoughtful, interested in all we do, respecting our individuality, skillful

in training us, wise in guidance, always available, helping us to find ourselves in maturity, integrity, and up-
rightness—is a thought which can have meaning for
everybody, whether we come to it by saying, "I had a
wonderful father, and I see that God is like that, only
more so," or by saying, "My Father disappointed me
here, and here, and here, but God, praise His name, will
be very different."[2]

As Packer points out, there is more than one way to
learn truth. If we were fortunate enough to see truth modeled before us, embracing correct teaching comes easier.
But we can also learn truth by contrast.

Realizing his own shortcomings as a father, author
Charlie Shedd reflects:

> One day when the time is right, I must say to my son:
> God is your heavenly Father and you can be glad that's
> true. I am your earthly father. But there is a big differ-
> ence. Your heavenly Father is like a perfect father. But
> since I am not, you must learn to contrast. Whenever I
> am the right kind of father, that's how God is. But when-
> ever I'm not, God is the opposite. Unless you remember
> this, you might not like God.[3]

When we understand how to use our father's failures,
these can change from stumbling blocks to springboards
that help us draw closer to our heavenly Father.

For example, if you suffered from any kind of fathering
deficit, sometimes hearing about a father like Sue's "dating
daddy" who introduced this chapter, you may feel a
twinge of envy. But you have nothing to resent. You *have*
a perfect Father, who has dozens of times spoken encouragement through the praises of His other children. Hearing
about dads like Sue's doesn't have to discourage us. It can

---

[2]J. I. Packer, *Knowing God* (Downer's Grove, Ill.: InterVarsity Press, 1973), 184.
[3]Charlie Shedd, *You Can Be a Great Parent* (Waco, Tex.: Word Books, 1970), 70.

rather be a stimulus to appreciate anew the wonderful Father we received when we came into God's family.

A Letter to Your Father-God

You might find help in an activity designed exclusively for women who didn't have perfect fathering. At the end of a presentation about fathers and daughters, I sometimes ask the audience to complete the following letter to God. It could be meaningful for you as well. Just read each statement, and finish it in a way that fits your life.

Dear Father,

I didn't belong to the family I was in by mere chance. You chose these people to teach me about you. Thank you for what I experienced with my dad of your fathering. One way he showed me your father-care was

_____

_____

Heavenly Father, we both know my earthly dad wasn't perfect. One way he failed to show me your father-care was_____

_____

_____

Father, you've been with me all through life. You are using the strengths and weaknesses of my relationship with my earthly father to draw me toward you. And you've been working to heal any wounds I carry from the fathering I experienced. Thank you for one way I've seen you fathering me by_____

_____

_____

Your daughter,

Being a Daughter of God

We've spent much time looking at our fathers as flesh-and-blood demonstrators of God's father-nature. But we look back at our earthly fathers so we can be free to move on to bonding with God. Philip implored Jesus, "Lord, show us the Father and that will be enough for us" (John 14:8). But he wasn't asking to see earthly fathering. Only the love and care of the heavenly Father genuinely satisfies.

And because I believe His love can satisfy our father hunger, I invite you to join me in affirming the words of the Heidelberg Catechism:

> The eternal Father of our Lord Jesus Christ,
>   who out of nothing created heaven and earth
>   and everything in them,
>   who still upholds and rules them
>   by his eternal counsel and providence,
> is my God and Father
>   because of Christ his Son.
>
> I trust him so much that I do not doubt
>   he will provide
>   whatever I need
>   for body and soul,
>   and he will turn to my good
>   whatever adversity he sends me
>   in this sad world.
> He is able to do this because he is almighty God.
> He desires to do it because he is a faithful Father.
> Amen.[4]

---

[4]Don Postema, *Space for God* (Grand Rapids, Mich.: Board of Publications of the Christian Reformed Church, 1983), 12.

◊ 14 ◊

Your Father Loves You:
A Devotional Journal

What is a Christian? The question can be answered in many ways, but the richest answer I know is that a Christian is one who has God for [her] Father.
                                        —J. I. Packer, in *Knowing God*

To grow closer to one you love, you need to know his thoughts, and allow him to know yours. This holds true for you and your heavenly Father, as well.

To that end, you'll find in the pages ahead fifteen devotional readings. Each begins with a passage of personality or character. The questions and thoughts that follow are designed to help you think more deeply about what He's shared of himself. The reading ends with a "prayer starter," an unfinished sentence prayer intended to help you share your heart with God in response.

As you share this time with your Father, "may your roots go down deep into the soil of His marvelous love; and may you be able to feel and understand, as all God's children should, how long, how wide, how deep, and how high this love really is; and to experience this love for yourselves" (Ephesians 3:17–18, TLB).

A Father You Can Relax With

God's Word to You:

"I bow my knees before the Father of our Lord Jesus Christ, for Whom every family in heaven and on earth is named—[that Father] from Whom all fatherhood takes its title and derives its name.

"May He grant you out of the rich treasury of His glory to be strengthened and reinforced with mighty power in the inner man by the Holy Spirit himself—indwelling your innermost being and personality.

"May Christ through your faith actually dwell—settle down, abide, make His permanent home—in your hearts!" (Ephesians 3:14–17a, AMP.).

To Think About:

Do you feel at home with your heavenly Father? When you get alone with Him, can you heave a sigh of relief, slip off your shoes, let down your guard, and relax in the sense of His love for you? He wants you to make yourself at home with Him.

A Prayer Starter:

Father, you do accept me, more than any person in my life ever could. When I picture you wanting to relax with me, I. . . .

A Loving Father

God's Word to You:

"May you be rooted deep in love and founded securely on love, that you may have the power and be strong to apprehend and grasp with all the saints (God's devoted people) the experience of that love, what is the breadth and length and height and depth of it; that you may really come to know—practically, through experience for yourselves—the love of Christ, which far surpasses mere knowledge without experience; that you may be filled through all your being unto all the fullness of God—that is, may have the richest measure of the divine Presence, and become a body wholly filled and flooded with God himself!" (Ephesians 3:17b–19, AMP.).

To Think About:

God loves you, and He isn't content that you simply grant intellectual assent to that fact. He wants you to *feel* His love, and have it flood your whole being. When were the times you most clearly felt God's love for you?

A Prayer Starter:

Father, when I hear you say you love me, I. . . .

A Father Who Wants You

God's Word to You:

"But when the right time came, the time God decided on, he sent his Son, born of a woman, born as a Jew, to buy freedom for us who were slaves to the law so that he could adopt us as his very own sons [and daughters]. And because we are his sons [and daughters] God has sent the Spirit of his Son into our hearts, so now we can rightly speak of God as our dear Father. Now we are no longer slaves, but God's own sons [and daughters]. And since we are his sons [and daughters], everything he has belongs to us, for that is the way God planned" (Galatians 4:4–7, TLB).

To Think About:

God has chosen you to be His daughter—not a servant girl, or an employee, or a distant relative, but His daughter. Can you imagine Him smiling at you and saying, "This is my beloved daughter, in whom I am well pleased"?

A Prayer Starter:

Father, calling you "Dad" seems. . . .

A Father Who Helps

God's Word to You:

"Everything has been entrusted to me by my Father. Only the Father knows the Son, and the Father is known only by the Son and by those to whom the Son reveals him.

"Come to me and I will give you rest—all of you who work so hard beneath a heavy yoke. Wear my yoke—for it fits perfectly—and let me teach you; for I am gentle and humble, and you shall find rest for your souls; for I give you only light burdens" (Matthew 11:27–30, TLB).

To Think About:

Your Father doesn't want you exhausted. He wants to give you rest. In what parts of your life might you let Him help you find rest?

A Prayer Starter:

Father, I feel exhausted and overwhelmed thinking about. . . .

A Father You Can Believe

God's Word to You:

"Do not be unequally yoked up with unbelievers. . . . What agreement can there be between a temple of God and idols? For we are the temple of the living God; even as God said, I will dwell in and with and among them and will walk in and with and among them and I will be their God, and they shall be my people.

"So, come out from among unbelievers, and separate (sever) yourselves from them, says the Lord, and touch not any unclean thing; then I will receive you kindly and treat you with favor, and I will be a Father to you, and you shall be my sons and daughters, says the Lord Almighty" (2 Corinthians 6:14, 16–18, AMP.).

To Think About:

God will not jam His love down our throats, or force us to receive His care. His love can take root only where it finds a seedbed of faith. We have to choose to believe what He says about himself, and when we do receive Him, He receives us as well. What makes it hard for you to believe Him when He says He really loves you?

A Prayer Starter:

Father, I try to picture myself opening my arms to receive you. When I do. . . .

A Welcoming Father

God's Word to You:

"For He says, In the time of favor (of an assured welcome) I have listened to and heeded your call, and I have helped you on the day of deliverance—the day of salvation. Behold, now is truly the time for a gracious welcome and acceptance of you from God; behold, now is the day of salvation!" (2 Corinthians 6:2, AMP.).

To Think About:

Right now God waits to welcome you into a warm and loving relationship with Him. If you still feel as though you can't return His smile and take His hand, why not? Is there a sin that needs confession? A wrong toward another that needs correction? Or simply unbelief that needs to be shoved aside so you can come to Him?

A Prayer Starter:

Father, you're glad to know me, and want to be close to me. When I realize how you feel, I. . . .

An Accepting Father

God's Word to You:

"For all who are led by the Spirit of God are sons [and daughters] of God. And so we should not be like cringing, fearful slaves, but we should behave like God's very own children, adopted into the bosom of His family, and calling to Him, 'Father, Father.'

"For his Holy Spirit speaks to us deep in our hearts, and tells us that we really are God's children. And since we are his children, we will share his treasures—for all God gives to his Son Jesus is now ours too. But if we are to share His glory, we must also share His suffering. Yet what we suffer now is nothing compared to the glory he will give us later" (Romans 8:14–18, TLB).

To Think About:

When we choose to let God love us, we're born into His family. And this new status as God's own daughter can't be taken from us, ever. Do you ever feel you're no longer good enough to be His daughter? Or that something you've done has caused God to change His mind about wanting you as His child? Your security depends on Him, not on you. You didn't earn your way into the family, and you can't disgrace your way out!

A Prayer Starter:

Father, I've felt unsure about belonging to you when. . . .

A Proud Father

God's Word to You:

"See how very much our heavenly Father loves us, for he allows us to be called his children—think of it—and we really are!" (1 John 3:1, TLB).

To Think About:

God doesn't squirm and roll His eyes when He has to claim you. He chose you as His daughter, and He is proud of His choice. He takes pleasure in you. What about you do you think pleases Him the most? In what ways do you especially delight Him? Have you asked Him?

A Prayer Starter:

Father, I like to think you smile when I. . . .

A Generous Father

God's Word to You:

"God showed how much he loved us by sending his only Son into this wicked world to bring to us eternal life through his death. In this act we see what real love is: it is not our love for God, but his love for us when he sent his Son to satisfy God's anger against our sins" (1 John 4:9–10, TLB).

To Think About:

God's affection for you isn't just talk. He proved His love by allowing Jesus to die in your place. Do you think of thanking Him for caring like this about you? Is there some personal way, some costly way, you might express your thanks? (Maybe it will be by giving love to someone in your life who doesn't deserve it.)

A Prayer Starter:

Father, you gave up the One you valued most for me. I want to thank you by. . . .

An Encouraging Father

God's Word to You:

"We know how much God loves us because we have felt his love and because we believe him when he tells us that he loves us dearly. God is love, and anyone who lives in love is living with God and God is living in him.

"And as we live with Christ, our love grows more perfect and complete; so we will not be ashamed and embarrassed at the day of judgment, but can face him with confidence and joy, because he loves us and we love him too" (1 John 4:16,17, TLB).

To Think About:

It isn't necessary to feel complete confidence in God's love. This scripture says our love grows more perfect and complete as we continue to live with Christ. In what ways have you seen growth in your love for God? What progress do you see in your experience of His love for you?

A Prayer Starter:

Father, I forget to realize that I'm growing. I'm not where I should be, but in some parts of life, I'm not where I was! Thank you for the growth you've given me in. . . .

A Father You Needn't Fear

God's Word to You:

"We need have no fear of someone who loves us perfectly; his perfect love for us eliminates all dread of what he might do to us. If we are afraid, it is for fear of what he might do to us, and shows that we are not fully convinced that he really loves us. So you see, our love for him comes as a result of his loving us first" (1 John 4:18–19, TLB).

To Think About:

Respect for God and worship of Him is what this scripture requires when we're admonished to "fear the Lord." But He never intends we cower before Him. This Father longs for obedience motivated by love, not terror. Are there times when you dread being with Him, and hide, as did Adam and Eve in the Garden, for fear of Him? He longs to clear away the obstacles between you.

A Prayer Starter:

Father, I feel afraid of you when. . . .

A Father Who Won't Leave

God's Word to You:

"Though my father and mother forsake me, the Lord will receive me" (Psalm 27:10, NIV).

To Think About:

Were you ever forsaken by your earthly father? Or if he was there physically, did you feel abandoned by him emotionally? With God, there is no "absent father syndrome," for His greatest present to us is His presence.

A Prayer Starter:

Father, will you always be with me? I. . . .

A Tender Father

God's Word to You:

"As a father has compassion on his children, so the Lord has compassion on those who fear him" (Psalm 103:13, NIV).

To Think About:

Compassion means "with feeling," or "feeling with," and this is your Father's heart toward you. There's no roughness or cruelty with Him. His heart is broken by the breaking of your heart. Your pains are His pains, your ecstasy His. Is it easy for you to believe God feels with you?

A Prayer Starter:

Father, the feeling I'd most like you to know about is. . . .

A Father Who Corrects

God's Word to You:

"Do not despise the Lord's discipline and do not resent his rebuke, because the Lord disciplines those he loves, as a father the son [or daughter] he delights in" (Proverbs 3:11, 12, NIV).

To Think About:

All of us are children who need help knowing right from wrong. And we don't have clear objectivity on our own shortcomings. Your heavenly Father does, however. He knows what needs correcting, and the best timing for that correction to take place. Is there some area of your life He wants to change in you now? Knowing where He wants to work allows you to work with Him, not against Him.

A Prayer Starter:

Father, you've been trying to discipline me in. . . .

A Father We Must Choose

God's Word to You:

"He came to that which belonged to Him—to His own domain, creation, things, world—and they who were His own did not receive Him and did not welcome Him.

"But to as many as did receive and welcome Him, He gave the authority (power, privilege, right) to become the children of God, that is, to those who believe in—adhere to, trust in and rely on—His name; who owe their birth neither to bloods, nor to the will of the flesh (that of physical impulses), nor to the will of man (that of a natural father), but to God.—They are born of God!" (John 1:11–13, AMP.).

To Think About:

In our earthly father, we didn't choose to be born, but that's not so in our heavenly family. God chose us to be His, but we have a say, as well. Have you chosen Him as your own dear Father, chosen to be born into His family?

A Prayer Starter:

Father, to welcome you requires that I step out onto a shadowed path where I cannot see what lies ahead. I can no longer control my destiny. All I see is you beside me, wanting to take my hand in yours. To your invitation, I say. . . .

Acknowledgments

Psychologists Dr. Kenneth Acheson, Dr. Robert Hutzell, Dr. John Musser, Dr. Bruce Narramore, Dr. Daniel Trobisch, and Dr. Paul Westmark graciously offered their professional perspectives on the issue of fathers and daughters. Bill Ewing helped in this capacity as well.

Loretta Miller and Paula Rinehart provided invaluable opportunities for me to present this material to their ministries. Hilda Epperson, Charette Barta, Traci Mullins, Carol Van Klompenberg, Martha Popson, the marvelous women of the Tuesday morning Bible study, and my husband Mike—all continued to believe in this project when the task seemed too big.

Lori Raymie lent an enthusiastic hand with research. David Christiansen at the Knoxville Community Hospital kindly offered work space.

And the women who talked with me about their fathers helped more than they know.